Here are u]
formulas To
sweeten life

Love

J UMBO
J ACK'S COOKBOOKS
AUDUBON MEDIA CORPORATION
301 BROADWAY · AUDUBON IA 50025
1-800-798-2635

THE ICE CREAM BOOK

ROY CAMPBELL

North Ferrisburgh, Vermont
1998

To My Aunt Nina

Now Just 92

In Whose Home Many Years Ago

I First Turned The Handle

Of An Ice Cream Maker

I would like to thank Kim Moirano who typed the manuscript, and who saw it through endless changes and revisions.

Also, special thanks to my publisher, Bruce Carlson, for accepting the manuscript, for his very knowledgeable assistance, and for his sense of humor.

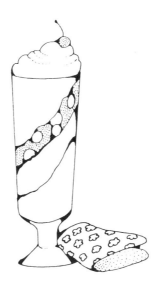

CONTENTS

PREFACE

This book began as an offshoot of a cookbook I wrote last year. That one contained a variety of ethnic and American dishes, and at the end I included a number of familiar ice cream flavors.

I decided to increase that number, but as time went by there were far too many to include in the book. However, I kept making more ice cream, as much from curiosity as from the pleasure in tasting new and unfamiliar flavor combinations. In a few weeks there were almost enough for a second book. I had about forty flavors then, and decided to keep on going.

In just over two months I reached 150, and had made enough. The freezer held many dozens of pints, and I gave it away as fast as possible to make room for more. By then all I could eat was a

little taste, one before freezing, one after, and

another the next day.

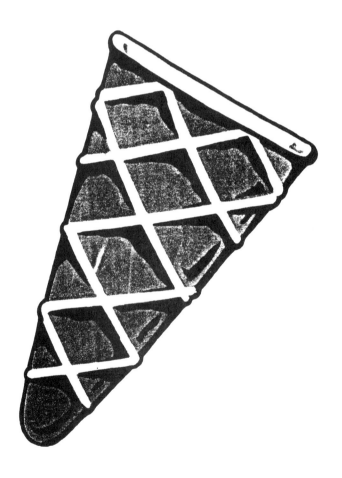

MAKING ICE CREAM

All of these ice creams are easy to make. This process is simple and quicker than any other I know of. There are no eggs in any of these recipes and therefore no heating, cooking and cooling of egg custards.

Instead, there is a dairy mix that consists of equal parts of half & half and heavy cream. The only exceptions being peanut butter and almond butter whose high oil content necessitates reducing the cream. This is done by substituting regular milk for 50 percent of the half and half, while keeping the heavy cream unchanged.

Basically all of the ingredients except the heavy cream and any added solids such as nuts, are put in a blender and blended at the highest speed for 30 seconds. The mixture is then transferred to the freezing container of your ice cream maker, and cooled in your home freezer for 20 minutes. The dasher or paddle should also be put in the freezer. Then, despite recommendations to the contrary in some sources, the heavy cream is separately whipped, added to the container, whipped briefly to blend, and frozen in your ice cream maker as directed. Afterwards any solid ingredients also pre-cooled in the freezer are stirred in, and the finished ice cream is transferred to a storage container.

Occasionally, depending on the initial temperature of the mixture there may be a little freezing of the liquid on the sides and bottom of the container while cooling in the freezer. If so, be sure to stir it back in with a rubber spatula, the indispensable tool in making ice cream. If you leave the mixture in the freezer for too long, or forget it altogether and the mixture freezes solid, just thaw it out. No harm is done.

I do not know why heavy cream is usually specified to be unwhipped, because whipping it beforehand guarantees that air gets incorporated into the ice cream as it is supposed to be. The churning motion of the dasher or paddle puts in very little air and certainly not enough to prevent most flavors from being too dense. Dense ice cream usually gets hard as a rock after a few days in the freezer. The heavy cream should be whipped until set but not stiff and the cream just barely falls off the beater blades.

If the freezing container of your ice cream making machine cannot fit in your home freezer, then leave the mixture in the blender to cool. And if neither fits in your home freezer, then put the mixture in a covered bowl to freeze for 20 minutes.

The purpose of pre-cooling the mixture is to reduce the churning time. Excess churning, like over whipping the heavy cream can lead to a dense greasy product.

While the time required to process the mixture varies from one machine to another, and depends on a number of factors, unless you plan to eat the ice cream right away, it is best if the ice cream is soft enough to roll slowly out of the machine and into a freezer container and settle properly. If it is stiff, then you will have to scrape it out and pack it down, and probably leave air space. If it is too soft or runny, the cream will probably separate and rise to the surface, and any added solids will sink to the bottom. So it is best to check it once or twice during the process, before the ice cream becomes too stiff.

All of these recipes yield about 1 ¾ quarts or 15 scoops of ice cream. Once you get the hang of putting these recipes together, you might want to make 1 quart instead of 2 quart batches. These recipes divide in half readily, and the precooling period is then reduced to 15 minutes. Remember, 1 ounce equals 2 level tablespoons and 1 level tablespoon equals 3 level teaspoons.

The freezing time for my ice and salt machine is reduced from about 25-30 minutes to 15-20 minutes.

I discovered that serving a variety of 4 or more flavors for dessert and using a melon baller instead of an ice cream scoop was a big hit with everyone.

You may find it convenient as I did to transfer the finished ice cream to 1 pint deli containers. Storage in the freezer is more convenient, and if you consume the ice cream over a period of time, opening and closing the lid of one large container many times affects the flavor and texture because the air and moisture are replaced frequently. A single pint makes a convenient gift, or special dessert when visiting friends.

It is also possible to make good ice cream even without an ice cream maker, since whipping the heavy cream beforehand guarantees enough air in the mixture. The problem is to get the ice cream frozen before the cream separates and rises. The solution is to put the ice cream mixture containing the heavy cream into a container or bowl and stir it a few times every 30 minutes, for about 2 hours. As the ice cream cools, it freezes on the outside first. After stirring in, the whole mixture cools gradually and eventually becomes too solid for the cream to rise. The time required for this process varies depending on the volume and contents of the ice cream mixture.

These recipes, one after the other are simple formulas and the individual instructions repeated throughout are complete in themselves. Some flavors differ only slightly from others, often only in one ingredient, or even only in the amount used of one ingredient. But each is unique and merits a listing by itself, and not merely as a variant of some other flavor.

THE INGREDIENTS

Every recipe here has some vanilla in it. Vanilla in small quantities acts as a masking agent for any possible undesirable buttery or excessive cream taste that can occur from over churning when the machine runs for too long, or from overwhipping the heavy cream, or sometimes even from the flavor of the cream itself. Use only pure vanilla extract. Imitation vanilla is a chemical that will guarantee you a truly inferior product. No other imitation flavor I know of can so degrade the taste of ice cream.

I always use pure extracts when available, but sometimes only flavorings are available. Extracts and flavorings are necessary because the natural unconcentrated form of juices are too weak when diluted 4 or 5 to 1 with the dairy mixture. Because of the very high water content in fruits and juices you quickly reach a limit then the ice cream texture becomes slushy like sherbert, and freezes hard as a rock.

Coconut for instance, is too mild a flavor in the canned cream or grated form. Adding too much of either makes a dense and oily or gritty ice cream. I use both flavoring and toasted sweetened flaked coconut and the two together work just fine. These flakes spread on a cookie sheet in the oven go from just right to burnt very quickly. When you get a whiff of coconut from the stove it is about done.

Maple syrup is a similar example. Pure maple syrup by itself is too weak when diluted in the cream, and adding more makes the ice cream too sweet. Yet still too weak in flavor. A little maple flavoring does the trick.

Another flavor with a different problem is rum. The alcohol is a strong enough flavor but it also acts as an anti-freeze and will make the ice cream mushy. I use less rum and add a little flavoring.

The citrus fruits, orange, lemon and lime alone or in combination yield a whole range of wonderful flavors. They fortunately have a built in solution, the rind. The fruit juice alone is insufficient, but the fine grated rind which is mashed and ground into the sugar beforehand releases the oils, which carry the essential flavor of the fruits. Together they are perfect.

The juice of lemon and lime are very acidic, and when added will expand the dairy mixture. But the ice cream in no way suffers. These three are amongst the most favored flavors of all and personally I've never had any of the three in a form so good and unexpected.

Chocolate is an extremely versatile flavor, second only to vanilla. Unsweetened cocoa, Dutch process is the proper form to use. Sweetened cocoa is fine stirred into hot milk, but it is mostly sugar and additives. The hard unsweetened bakers chocolate has lots more oil than cocoa and must be stirred in atop a double boiler almost endlessly for it to dissolve. These chocolate recipes call for 2 or 3 ounces of cocoa, and you will definitely notice the difference in color and taste, similar to the difference between milk chocolate and dark chocolate candy. Two ounces seem best in combination with other flavors, while 3 ounces is fine in chocolate alone or combined with a particularly robust flavor, like rum or clove. If you use 3 ounces with the denser depth of flavor be sure to boost the other flavors or they will be weak and barely detectable.

For coffee use only fresh brewed, preferably fresh roasted and ground too, but never instant. Espresso has a rather harsh flavor, and does not go so well with other flavors.

Bananas go well with lots of other flavors but if the fruit is too ripe it will overwhelm most of them. To measure bananas or any whole or sliced fruit, fill a measuring cup half full with the half & half, and add pieces of the fruit until the liquid rises to the desired level.

Pineapple is available in a frozen juice concentrate and works just fine. The juice, fresh or canned is too weak.

Nuts are optional and are used when a particular flavor seems to call for them. After roasting, cool the nuts in the freezer, for if they are at room temperature when added to the finished ice cream, they can melt their way down. Be careful toasting pine nuts, they, like coconut flakes go from just right to burnt very quickly. Again, when you get a whiff of them from the oven they are done, and they will be light tan. When brown, they are too strong and resinous.

In a pinch you can sprinkle more sugar into the mixture and whip it before freezing if you need to. Ice cream tastes sweeter before you freeze it.

For many people who have only had store bought ice cream, whatever the highly variable quality of commercial mixes, this ice cream will be an awakening as to how good the real thing is.

Of the 150 flavors here, most were put into 1 pint containers and given to dozens of people. They found it to be the best they ever tasted. Follow the directions carefully and I think you will too.

LEMON

1 pint heavy cream
1 pint half & half
1 teaspoon pure vanilla extract
1 ¼ cups of sugar
1 teaspoon fine grated lemon rind
½ cup fresh squeezed lemon juice

Take 1 tablespoon of the sugar and the rind, and using a mortar and pestle, or with a custard cup or small glass and wooden spoon handle, mash and grind them together until the rind is further broken up and the sugar turns yellow.

In a blender combine all of the ingredients except the heavy cream and blend at highest speed for 30 seconds. Transfer the mixture to the freezing container and put it in the freezer for 20 minutes.

Then, separately whip the heavy cream until set but not stiff and the cream barely falls off the beater blades. Add the whipped cream to the container and whip briefly to blend. Freeze as directed.

This is a real delight, sweet and tangy with a silky texture probably caused by the effect of the acid on the cream. It is truly the creme de la creme of any dessert made with lemon. Not to be compared to the overly sweet goo that fills lemon meringue pies. **24**

CHOCOLATE MAPLE WALNUT

1 pint heavy cream
1 pint half & half
1 teaspoon pure vanilla extract
½ cup sugar
½ cup pure maple syrup
½ teaspoon maple flavoring
2 ounces unsweetened cocoa
½ cup chopped walnuts

Put the walnuts in the freezer. In a blender combine all of the other ingredients except the heavy cream and nuts, and blend at highest speed for 30 seconds. Transfer the mixture to the freezing container and put it in the freezer for 20 minutes.

Then, separately whip the heavy cream until set but not stiff and the cream just barely falls off the beater blades. Add the whipped cream to the container and whip briefly to blend. Freeze as directed. When complete, remove the dasher or paddle, stir in the walnuts, and transfer to a freezer container.

This brings the old favorite maple walnut a big step higher.

CINNAMON PEACH

1 pint heavy cream
1 pint half & half
½ teaspoon pure vanilla extract
¾ cup sugar
½ teaspoon cinnamon
1 ½ cups fresh peaches, peeled and sliced

In a blender put all of the ingredients, except the heavy cream and blend at highest speed for 30 seconds. Transfer the mixture to the freezing container and put it in the freezer.

After 20 minutes, separately whip the heavy cream until set but not stiff and the cream just barely falls off the beater blades. Add the whipped cream to the container and whip briefly to blend. Freeze as directed.

CONCORD GRAPE

1 pint heavy cream
1 pint half & half
½ teaspoon pure vanilla extract
3 ounces sugar
¾ cup frozen concord juice concentrate

In a blender put all of the ingredients except the heavy cream and blend at highest speed for 30 seconds. Transfer the mixture to the freezing container and put it in the freezer for 20 minutes.

Then, separately whip the heavy cream until set but not stiff and the cream just barely falls off the beater blades. Add the whipped cream to the container and whip briefly to blend. Freeze as directed.

This is a very interesting flavor. It is quite similar in color and taste to both blueberry and black raspberry, but with a bit of a bite as you swallow. In any event no one will guess what the flavor is.

ORANGE PINEAPPLE

1 pint heavy cream
1 pint half & half
1 teaspoon pure vanilla extract
¾ cup sugar
1 teaspoon fine grated orange rind firmly packed
¾ cup frozen pineapple juice concentrate

Take 1 tablespoon of the sugar and the rind and using a mortar and pestle, or with a custard cup or small glass and wooden spoon handle, mash and grind them together until the rind is further broken up and the sugar turns orange.

Put all of the ingredients except the heavy cream in a blender and run it at highest speed for 30 seconds. Transfer the mixture to the freezing container and put it in the freezer for 20 minutes.

Then, separately whip the heavy cream until set but not stiff and the cream just barely falls off the beater blades. Add the whipped cream to the container and whip briefly to blend. Freeze as directed.

This is a favorite flavor of childhood, that seems to have disappeared in recent years. Everyone loves it.

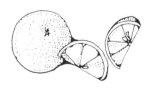

COCONUT RUM

1 pint heavy cream
1 pint half & half
½ teaspoon pure vanilla extract
¾ cup sugar
½ teaspoon (scant) coconut flavoring
4 tablespoons dark rum

Put all of the ingredients except the heavy cream into a blender and run at highest speed for 30 seconds. Transfer the mixture to the freezing container and put it in the freezer.

After 20 minutes, separately whip the heavy cream until set but not stiff and the cream just barely falls off the beater blades. Add the whipped cream to the container and whip briefly to blend. Freeze as directed.

CANTALOUPE

1 pint heavy cream
1 pint half & half
½ teaspoon pure vanilla extract
5 ounces sugar
1 ½ cups cantaloupe

Put all of ingredients except the heavy cream in a blender and blend at the highest speed for 30 seconds. Transfer the mixture to the freezing container and put it in the freezer.

After 20 minutes, separately whip the heavy cream until set but not stiff and the cream just barely falls off the beater blades. Add the whipped cream to the container and whip briefly to blend. Freeze as directed.

ORANGE CHOCOLATE

1 pint heavy cream
1 pint half & half
1 teaspoon pure vanilla extract
1 cup sugar
1 teaspoon fine grated orange rind firmly
packed
6 ounces fresh squeezed orange juice
2 ounces unsweetened cocoa

Take 1 tablespoon of the sugar and the rind, and using a mortar and pestle, or with a custard cup or small glass and wooden spoon handle, mash and grind them together until the rind is further broken up and the sugar turns orange.

Put all of the ingredients except the heavy cream into a blender and blend at highest speed for 30 seconds. Transfer the mixture to the freezing container and put it in the freezer.

After 20 minutes, separately whip the heavy cream until set but not stiff, and the cream just barely falls off the beater blades. Add the whipped cream to the container and whip briefly to blend. Freeze as directed.

This is a great flavor evoked by the memory of a familiar candy bar.

BUTTER PECAN

1 pint heavy cream
1 pint half & half
1 teaspoon pure vanilla extract
2 tablespoons sugar
¾ cup light brown sugar, firmly packed
3 tablespoons butter
¾ cup pecan halves, roasted for 15 minutes
at 275°

Put the roasted pecans in the freezer.

In a sauce pan on medium heat add the butter and brown sugar and stir them together until the mixture begins to bubble and puff a bit. Cook with constant stirring for about 4 minutes (235° - 240° on candy thermometer) and remove from heat.

Put all of the ingredients except the heavy cream and pecans in a blender and run at highest speed for 30 seconds. Transfer the mixture to the freezing container and put it in the freezer for 20 minutes.

Then, separately whip the heavy cream until set but not stiff and cream just barely falls off the beater blades. Add the whipped cream to the container and whip briefly to blend. Freeze as directed. When complete, remove the dasher or paddle and stir in the pecans with a spatula and transfer the ice cream to a freezer container.

Cooking the butter and brown sugar together makes a world of difference to this flavor as you will discover.

GINGER PEACH

1 pint heavy cream
1 pint half & half
1 teaspoon pure vanilla extract
1 cup sugar
¾ teaspoon fine grated ginger
1 ½ cups fresh peaches, pitted, peeled and sliced

Put all of the ingredients except the heavy cream into a blender and run at highest speed for 30 seconds. Transfer the mixture to the freezing container and put it in the freezer.

After 25 minutes, separately whip the heavy cream until set but not stiff and the cream just barely falls off the beater blades.

Add the whipped cream to the container and whip briefly to blend. Freeze as directed.

PEANUT BUTTER BANANA

1 pint heavy cream
1 pint half & half
1 teaspoon pure vanilla extract
¾ cup sugar
3 ounces non-homogenized peanut butter
4 ounces banana, ripe but firm, with brown spots on the skin but not on the fruit

Put all of the ingredients except the heavy cream into a blender and blend at highest speed for 30 seconds. Transfer the mixture to the freezing container and put it in the freezer for 20 minutes.

Then, separately whip the heavy cream until set, but not stiff and the cream just barely falls off the beater blades. Add the whipped cream to the container and whip briefly to blend. Freeze as directed.

This is an unusual flavor but a delight to those of us who once ate bananas and peanut butter sandwiches, or perhaps still do.

RASPBERRY

1 pint heavy cream
1 pint half & half
1 ½ teaspoons pure vanilla extract
1 ¼ cups sugar
1 ½ cups raspberries, fresh or whole unsweetened frozen

In a blender combine all of the ingredients except the heavy cream, and blend at highest speed for 30 seconds. Transfer the mixture to the freezing container and put it in the freezer for 20 minutes.

Then, separately whip the heavy cream until set but not stiff, and the cream just barely falls off the beater blades. Add the whipped cream to the container and whip briefly to blend. Freeze as directed.

You can use the identical proportions here to make black raspberry, blackberry, and boysenberry ice cream. If you use fresh berries which are sweeter, reduce the sugar content to one cup.

CHOCOLATE ANISE WITH TOASTED PINE NUTS

1 pint heavy cream
1 pint half & half
1 teaspoon pure vanilla extract
¾ cup sugar
2 ounces unsweetened cocoa
1 teaspoon anise extract
3 ounces pine nuts, toasted in a 275° oven for 6-10 minutes

Put the toasted pine nuts in the freezer. In a blender combine all of the ingredients except the heavy cream and nuts, and blend at the highest speed for 30 seconds. Transfer the mixture to the freezing container and put it in the freezer for 25 minutes.

Then, separately whip the heavy cream until set but not stiff and the cream just barely falls off the beater blades. Add the whipped cream to the container and whip briefly to blend. Freeze as directed.

When complete, remove the dasher or paddle and stir in the pine nuts with a spatula, and transfer the finished ice cream to a freezer container.

BANANA LIME

1 pint heavy cream
1 pint half & half
1 teaspoon pure vanilla extract
⅞ cup sugar
½ teaspoon fine grated lemon rind, firmly
packed
2 tablespoons fresh squeezed lime juice
1 cup banana, ripe but firm with brown spots
on the skin but not on the fruit

Take 1 tablespoon of the sugar and the rind, and using a mortar and pestle, or with a custard cup or small glass and wooden spoon handle, mash and grind them together until the rind is further broken up and the sugar turns green.

Add all of the ingredients except the heavy cream to a blender and run at highest speed for 30 seconds. Put the mixture into the freezing container and place it in the freezer.

After 20 minutes, separately whip the heavy cream until set but not stiff and the cream just barely falls off the beater blades. Add the whipped cream to the container and whip briefly to blend. Freeze as directed.

PEPPERMINT MOLASSES

1 pint heavy cream
1 pint half & half
½ teaspoon pure vanilla extract
3 ounces sugar   34

2 ounces unsulphured molasses
½ teaspoon peppermint extract

Put all of the ingredients except the heavy cream in a blender and blend at highest speed for 30 seconds. Transfer the mixture to the freezing container and put it in the freezer.

After 20 minutes, separately whip the heavy cream until set but not stiff and the cream just barely falls off the beater blades. Add the whipped cream to the container and whip briefly to blend. Freeze as directed.

After using both of these flavors in many combinations that worked so well, I decided to combine them. The taste reminds me of a candy long since forgotten.

ORANGE VANILLA

1 pint heavy cream
1 pint half & half
2 teaspoons pure vanilla extract
¾ cup sugar
1 ½ teaspoons fine grated orange rind, firmly packed
4 ounces fresh squeezed orange juice

Take 1 tablespoon of the sugar and the rind, and using a mortar and pestle, or with a custard cup or small glass and wooden spoon handle, mash and grind them together until the rind is further broken up and the sugar turns orange.

In a blender combine all of the ingredients except the heavy cream and blend at highest speed for 30 seconds. Transfer the mixture to the freezing container and put it in the freezer for 20 minutes.

Then, separately whip the heavy cream until set but not stiff, and the cream just barely falls off the beater blades. Add the whipped cream to the container and whip briefly to blend. Freeze as directed.

This flavor was inspired by the memory of creamsicles which were once a favorite but this is even better.

PEANUT BUTTER

1 pint heavy cream
½ pint half & half
½ pint regular milk
1 teaspoon pure vanilla extract
1 cup sugar
3 ounces non-homogenized peanut butter

In a blender combine all of the ingredients except the heavy cream and blend at higher speed for 30 seconds. Transfer the mixture to the freezing container and put it in the freezer.

After 20 minutes, separately whip the heavy cream until set but not stiff and the cream just barely falls off the beater blades. Add the whipped cream to the container and whip briefly to blend. Freeze as directed.

The density of peanut butter makes it necessary to reduce the cream content of the dairy base by substituting some milk. The flavor is very full and rich, and hugely satisfying to those of us who love real peanut butter.

HONEY LEMON

1 pint heavy cream
1 pint half & half
½ teaspoon pure vanilla extract
2 ounces sugar
3 ounces honey
1 teaspoon fine grated lemon rind firmly packed

Take 1 tablespoon of the sugar and the rind, and with a mortar and pestle, or using a custard cup or small glass and wooden spoon handle, mash and grind them together until the rind is further broken up and the sugar turns yellow.

In a blender put all of the ingredients except the heavy cream and blend at highest speed for 30 seconds. Transfer the mixture to the freezing container and put it in the freezer for 20 minutes.

Then, separately whip the heavy cream until set but not stiff and the cream just barely falls off the beater blades. Add the whipped cream to the container mix and whip briefly to blend.

Freeze as directed.

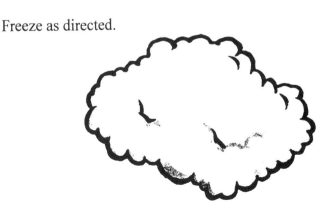

MOCHA ALMOND

1 pint heavy cream
1 pint half & half
1 teaspoon pure vanilla extract
1 ⅛ cups sugar
2 ounces unsweetened cocoa
6 ounces double strength fresh brewed coffee
3 ounces almond butter

Add 2 coffee measures (4 level tablespoons) of ground coffee to 8 ounces of boiling water and stir. Let the coffee steep for 3 minutes and filter.

In a blender put 6 ounces of the filtered coffee and all of the other ingredients except the heavy cream, and blend at highest speed for 30 seconds. Transfer the mixture to the freezing container and put it in the freezer for 20 minutes.

Then separately whip the heavy cream until set but not stiff and the cream just barely falls off the beater blades. Add the whipped cream to the container mix and whip briefly to blend.

Freeze as directed.

LEMON & LIME

1 pint heavy cream
1 pint half & half
1 teaspoon pure vanilla extract
1 ¼ cups sugar
1 teaspoon fine grated lemon rind, firmly packed
½ teaspoon fine grated lime rind, firmly packed
2 ounces fresh squeezed lemon juice
2 ounces fresh squeezed lime juice

Take 1 tablespoon of the sugar and both rinds, and using a mortar and pestle, or with a custard cup or small glass and wooden spoon handle, mash and grind them together until the rind is further broken up and the sugar turns yellow green.

Put all of the ingredients except the heavy cream into a blender and run at the highest speed for 30 seconds. Transfer the mixture to the freezing container and put it in the freezer.

After 20 minutes, separately whip the heavy cream until set but not stiff and the cream just barely falls off the beater blades. Add the whipped cream to the container and whip briefly to blend. Freeze as directed.

This is a supreme flavor, not to be compared to any other lemon and lime combination you have had.

BANANA COCONUT

1 pint heavy cream
1 pint half & half
1 teaspoon pure vanilla extract
¾ cup sugar
½ teaspoon (scant) coconut flavoring
6 ounces banana, firm but ripe with brown
spots on the skin but not on the fruit
½ cup flaked sweetened coconut toasted in a
300° oven for 6-8 minutes

Put the toasted coconut in the freezer. In a
blender, combine all of the ingredients except the heavy
cream and toasted coconut and blend at highest speed for
30 seconds. Transfer the mixture to the freezing container
and put it in the freezer for 20 minutes.

Then, separately whip the heavy cream until set
but not stiff and the cream just barely falls off the beater
blades. Add the whipped cream to the container and whip
briefly to blend. Freeze as directed. When complete,
remove the dasher or paddle, stir in the coconut with a
spatula, and transfer the ice cream to a freezer container.

CHOCOLATE ORANGE PINEAPPLE

1 pint heavy cream
1 pint half & half
1 teaspoon pure vanilla extract
⅞ cup sugar
2 ounces unsweetened cocoa
1 teaspoon fine grated orange rind, firmly
packed
6 ounces frozen pineapple juice concentrate

Take 1 tablespoon of the sugar and the rind, and using a mortar and pestle, or with a custard cup or small glass and wooden spoon handle, mash and grind them together until the rind is further broken up and the sugar turns orange.

In a blender add all of the ingredients except the heavy cream and blend at highest speed for 30 seconds. Transfer and put it in the freezer for 20 minutes.

Then, separately whip the heavy cream until set but not stiff and the cream just barely falls off the beater blades. Add the whipped cream to the container and whip briefly to blend. Freeze as directed.

This flavor goes orange pineapple one better and chocolate lovers will love the improvement.

PEANUT BUTTER MALT

1 pint heavy cream
1 pint half & half
1 teaspoon pure vanilla extract
¾ cup sugar
2 ounces malt powder
3 ounces non-homogenized peanut butter

In a blender put all of the ingredients except the heavy cream, and blend at highest speed for 30 seconds. Transfer the mixture to the freezing container and put it in the freezer.

After 20 minutes, separately whip the heavy cream until set but not stiff, and the cream just barely falls off the beater blades. Add the whipped cream to the container and whip briefly to blend. Freeze as directed.

LEMON PEACH

1 pint heavy cream
1 pint half & half
½ teaspoon pure vanilla extract
¾ cup sugar
¾ teaspoon fine grated lemon rind, firmly packed
1 ½ cups fresh peaches peeled and sliced

Take 1 tablespoon of the sugar and the rind, and using a mortar and pestle, or with a custard cup or small glass and wooden spoon handle, mash and grind them together until the rind is further broken up and the sugar turns yellow.

Put all of the ingredients except the heavy cream into a blender and blend at highest speed for 30 seconds. Transfer the mixture to the freezing container and put it in the freezer.

After 20 minutes, separately whip the heavy cream until set but not stiff and the cream just barely falls off the beater blades. Add the whipped cream to the container and whip briefly to blend. Freeze as directed.

MANGO

1 pint heavy cream
1 pint half & half
½ teaspoon pure vanilla extract
¾ cup sugar
1 ½ cups fresh mango fruit peeled and sliced

In a blender put all of the ingredients except the heavy cream and blend at highest speed for 30 seconds.

Transfer the mixture to the freezing container and put it in the freezer for 20 minutes.

Then, separately whip the heavy cream until set but not stiff and the cream just barely falls off the beater blades. Add the whipped cream to the container and whip briefly to blend. Freeze as directed.

CHOCOLATE HONEY ALMOND

1 pint heavy cream
1 pint half & half
1 teaspoon pure vanilla extract
2 ounces sugar
3 ounces honey
2 ounces unsweetened cocoa
3 ounces almond butter

Put all of the ingredients except the heavy cream into a blender and blend at highest speed for 30 seconds. Transfer the mixture to the freezing container and put it in the freezer for 20 minutes.

Then, separately whip the heavy cream until set but not stiff, and the cream just barely falls off the beater blades. Add the whipped cream to the container mix and whip briefly to blend. Freeze as directed.

This trio of flavors is an exceptional blend that all come through simultaneously as you taste it. It is also very easy to make.

CARDAMON

1 pint heavy cream
1 pint half & half
1 teaspoon pure vanilla extract
¾ cup sugar
1 teaspoon cardamon powder, from fresh ground seeds
⅓ cup pine nuts, toasted in a 275° oven for 6-10 minutes

Put the toasted pine nuts in the freezer. Grind the seeds very fine in a mortar and pestle or with an electric grinder. This recipe will require about 20 cardamon pods worth of seeds. Be sure to remove before grinding the white fibrous material in the pods, and to use black and shiny seeds. When the seeds dry out, they become brown and powdery and lose much of their flavor.

Put all of the ingredients except the heavy cream and nuts in a blender and blend at highest speed for 30 seconds. Transfer the mixture to the freezing container and put it in the freezer.

After 20 minutes, separately whip the heavy cream until set but not stiff and the cream just barely falls off the beater blades. Add the whipped cream to the container and whip briefly to blend. Freeze as directed. When complete, remove the dasher or paddle and stir in the pine nuts with a spatula, and transfer the ice cream to a freezer container.

APPLESAUCE CINNAMON

1 pint heavy cream
1 pint half & half
½ teaspoon pure vanilla extract
¾ cup plus 1 tablespoon sugar
½ teaspoon cinnamon
2 pounds apples, 8 small or 4 large quartered
⅓ cup water

In a sauce pan put the water, apples, cinnamon and 1 tablespoon of the sugar and cook on low heat until the apples are all mashed up, in about 10 minutes. Force the pulp through a strainer with a wooden spoon and let the applesauce cool. The yield will vary a bit, but for the ice cream use just 1 ½ cups.

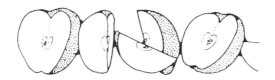

Put all of the ingredients except the heavy cream into a blender and blend at highest speed for 30 seconds. Transfer the mixture to the freezing container and put it in the freezer.

After 20 minutes, separately whip the heavy cream until set but not stiff, and the cream just barely falls off the beater blades. Add the whipped cream to the container and whip briefly to blend. Freeze as directed.

This takes a bit of preparation but is worth it. My applesauce is improved by becoming an ice cream.

MOCHA BUTTER PECAN

1 pint heavy cream
1 pint half & half
1 teaspoon pure vanilla extract
3 ounces sugar
3 tablespoons butter
¾ cup firm packed light brown sugar
2 ounces unsweetened cocoa
6 ounces double strength fresh brewed coffee
¾ cup pecan halves, roasted at 275° for 15
minutes

Put the roasted pecans in the freezer. Add 2 coffee measures (4 level tablespoons) of ground coffee to 8 ounces of boiling water and stir. Let the coffee steep for 3 minutes and filter.

In a small sauce pan on medium heat mix and stir the butter and brown sugar for about 4 or 5 minutes. The mixture will bubble and puff as it cooks. The temperature if you have a candy thermometer will be 236° - 240° degrees. Turn the heat off. In a blender add 6 ounces of the coffee, the half & half, vanilla, sugar, and cocoa, and blend at highest speed for 10 seconds. Then, with the blender still running, scrape the butter and brown sugar into the blender and let it run for 30 seconds. Transfer the mixture to the freezing container and put it in the freezer for 20 minutes.

Then, separately whip the heavy cream until set but not stiff, and the cream just barely falls off the beater blades. Add the whipped cream to the container mix and whip briefly to blend. Freeze as directed. When complete, remove the dasher or paddle and stir in the pecans with a spatula and transfer the ice cream to a freezer container.

Adding the coffee and chocolate taste of mocha to this old standard really hits the spot.

COCONUT ORANGE

1 pint heavy cream
1 pint half & half
1 teaspoon pure vanilla extract
1 cup sugar
1 ½ teaspoons fine grated orange rind, firmly packed
4 ounces fresh squeezed orange juice
½ teaspoon coconut flavoring
½ cup flaked sweetened coconut toasted in a 300° oven for 6-8 minutes

Put the toasted coconut in the freezer. Take 1 tablespoon of the sugar and the rind, and using a mortar and pestle, or with a custard cup or small glass and wooden spoon handle, mash and grind them together until the rind is further broken up and the sugar turns orange.

Combine all of the ingredients except the heavy cream in a blender, and blend at highest speed for 30 seconds. Transfer the mixture to the freezing container and put it in the freezer.

After 20 minutes, separately whip the heavy cream until set but not stiff and the cream just barely falls off the beater blades. Add the whipped cream to the container and whip briefly to blend. Freeze as directed. When complete, remove the dasher or paddle, stir in the coconut with a spatula, and transfer the ice cream to a freezer container.

GINGER MOLASSES

1 pint heavy cream
1 pint half & half
2 teaspoons pure vanilla extract
5 ounces sugar
2 ounces unsulphured molasses
2 teaspoons fine grated ginger

Combine all of the ingredients except the heavy cream in a blender and blend at highest speed for 30 seconds. Transfer the mixture to the freezing container and put in the freezer.

After 20 minutes, separately whip the heavy cream until set but not stiff, and the cream just barely falls off the beater blades. Add the whipped cream to the container and whip briefly to blend. Freeze as directed.

Molasses, when it's not straight out of the jar is very appealing. The diluted flavor combined with fresh ginger works to make an unusual combination.

PEPPERMINT PEACH

1 pint heavy cream
1 pint half & half
1 teaspoon pure vanilla extract
¾ cup sugar
½ teaspoon peppermint extract
1 ½ cups fresh peaches, pitted, peeled and sliced

Combine all of the ingredients except the heavy cream in a blender, and run at highest speed for 30 seconds. Transfer the mixture to the freezing container and put it in the freezer.

After 20 minutes, separately whip the heavy cream until set but not stiff, and the cream just barely falls off the beater blades. Add the whipped cream to the container and whip briefly to blend. Freeze as directed.

ORANGE WITH TOASTED PINE NUTS

1 pint heavy cream
1 pint half & half
1 teaspoon pure vanilla extract
1 ¼ cups sugar
1 ½ teaspoons fine grated orange rind, firmly packed
6 ounces fresh squeezed orange juice
3 ounces pine nuts toasted in a 275° oven for 6-10 minutes

Put the toasted pine nuts in the freezer. Take 1 tablespoon of the sugar and the rind, and using a mortar and pestle, or with a custard cup or small glass and wooden spoon handle, mash and grind them together until the rind is further broken up and the sugar turns orange.

In a blender combine all of the ingredients except the heavy cream and nuts, and blend at highest speed for 30 seconds. Transfer the mixture to the freezing container and put it in the freezer for 20 minutes.

Then, separately whip the heavy cream until set but not stiff, and the cream just barely falls off the beater blades. Add the whipped cream to the container and whip briefly to blend. Freeze as directed. When complete, remove the dasher or paddle and stir in the pine nuts with a spatula, and transfer the ice cream to a freezer container.

CHOCOLATE CINNAMON

1 pint heavy cream
1 pint half & half
1 teaspoon pure vanilla extract
⅞ cup sugar
1 teaspoon cinnamon
2 ounces unsweetened cocoa

Combine all of the ingredients in a blender except the heavy cream and blend at the highest speed for 30 seconds. Transfer the mixture to the freezing container and put it in the freezer.

After 20 minutes, separately whip the heavy cream until set but not stiff, and the cream just barely falls off the beater blades. Add the whipped cream to the container and whip briefly to blend. Freeze as directed.

PECAN

1 pint heavy cream
1 pint half & half
1 teaspoon pure vanilla extract
¾ cup sugar
¾ cup pecans, roasted in a 275° oven for 15 minutes

Put all of the ingredients except the heavy cream into a blender and blend at highest speed for 30 seconds. Transfer the mixture to the freezing container and put it in the freezer.

After 20 minutes, separately whip the heavy cream until set but not stiff, and the cream just barely falls off the beater blades. Add the whipped cream to the container and whip briefly to blend. Freeze as directed.

I don't know whether or not they make pecan butter, but after this goes in the blender that's what you get. And what a delicious and unexpected flavor for all those who love pecans.

HONEY PINEAPPLE

1 pint heavy cream
1 pint half & half
1 teaspoon pure vanilla extract
2 ounces sugar
3 ounces honey
6 ounces frozen pineapple juice concentrate

Combine all of the ingredients except the heavy cream in a blender at highest speed for 30 seconds. Transfer the mixture to the freezing container and put it in the freezer.

After 20 minutes, separately whip the heavy cream until set but not stiff, and the cream just barely falls off the beater blades. Add the whipped cream to the container and whip briefly to blend. Freeze as directed.

MOCHA RUM WITH WALNUTS

1 pint heavy cream
1 pint half & half
1 teaspoon pure vanilla extract
⅞ cup sugar
2 ounces unsweetened cocoa
6 ounces double strength fresh brewed coffee
½ teaspoon rum flavoring
1 tablespoon dark rum
½ cup chopped walnuts

Put the walnuts in the freezer. Take 2 coffee measures (4 level tablespoons), and add to 8 ounces of boiling water and stir. Let steep for 3 minutes and filter.

Put 6 ounces of the coffee and all of the other ingredients except the heavy cream and nuts, into a blender and run at highest speed for 30 seconds. Transfer the mixture to the freezing container and put it in the freezer.

After 20 minutes, whip the heavy cream until set but not stiff, and the cream just barely falls off the beater blades. Add the whipped cream to the container and whip briefly to blend. Freeze as directed. When complete,

remove the dasher or paddle and stir in the walnuts with a spatula and transfer the ice cream to a freezing container.

LEMON PINEAPPLE

1 pint heavy cream
1 pint half & half
1 teaspoon pure vanilla extract
¾ cup sugar
1 teaspoon fine grated lemon rind, firmly packed
¾ cup frozen pineapple juice concentrate

Take 1 tablespoon of the sugar and the rind, and using a mortar and pestle, or with a custard cup or small glass and wooden spoon handle, mash and grind them together until the rind is further broken up and the sugar turns yellow.

In a blender combine all of the ingredients except the heavy cream and blend at highest speed for 30 seconds. Transfer the mixture to the freezing container and put it in the freezer for 20 minutes.

Then, separately whip the heavy cream until set but not stiff, and the cream just barely falls off the beater blades. Add the whipped cream to the container and whip briefly to blend.

After orange pineapple this one seemed obvious but I've never seen it before. The two tart flavors together are quite unique, and many people prefer it to the other flavor.

CRANBERRY

1 pint heavy cream
1 pint half & half
½ teaspoon pure vanilla extract

1 ¼ cups sugar
2 - 12 ounce packages whole cranberries

Pick over the cranberries and discard any that are brown or withered or mushy. Put the remainder in a pot on low heat; and cook and mash them until the berries become a mass of skin and thick pulp. Put the pulp into a strainer and force it through until you have mostly skin left. Be sure to scrape off any pulp on the outside of the strainer. The yield will be about 1 ½ cups.

In a blender combine all of the ingredients except the heavy cream and blend at highest speed for 30 seconds. Transfer the mixture to the freezing container and put it in the freezer.

After 20 minutes, separately whip the heavy cream until set but not stiff, and the cream just barely falls off the beater blades. Add the whipped cream to the mix and whip briefly to blend. Freeze as directed.

CHOCOLATE MOLASSES PEANUT BUTTER

1 pint heavy cream
1 pint half & half
1 teaspoon pure vanilla extract
4 ounces sugar
2 ounces unsweetened cocoa
2 ounces unsulphured molasses
3 ounces non-homogenized peanut butter

Put all of the ingredients except the heavy cream into a blender and run at highest speed for 30 seconds.

Transfer the mixture to the freezing container and put it in the freezer for 20 minutes.

Then, separately whip the heavy cream until set but not stiff, and cream just barely falls off the beater blades. Add the whipped cream to the container and whip briefly to blend. Freeze as directed.

The combination of this trio of flavors is reminiscent of an old candy bar, but I can't remember which one.

GOLDEN RAISIN

1 pint heavy cream
1 pint half & half
1 teaspoon pure vanilla extract
3 ounces sugar
¾ cup golden raisins firm packed
¾ cup boiling water

Pour the boiling water over the raisins and let them steep for 5 minutes. Stir a few times. Put all of the ingredients except the heavy cream into a blender and blend at highest speed for 30 seconds. Transfer the mixture to the freezing container and put it in the freezer for 20 minutes.

Then, separately whip the heavy cream until set but not stiff and the cream just barely falls off the beater blades. Add the whipped cream to the container and whip briefly to blend. Freeze as directed.

CINNAMON PEPPERMINT

1 pint heavy cream
1 pint half & half
½ teaspoon pure vanilla extract
¾ cup sugar
1 ½ teaspoons cinnamon
1 teaspoon peppermint extract

Put all of the ingredients except the heavy cream into a blender and blend at highest speed for 30 seconds. Transfer the mixture to the freezing container and put it in the freezer for 20 minutes.

Then, separately whip the heavy cream until set but not stiff, and the cream just barely falls off the beater blades. Add the whipped cream to the container and whip briefly to blend. Freeze as directed.

When the combination first came to mind I wondered if perhaps it might taste like a cross between toothpaste and mouthwash. But everyone seems to love it, especially kids.

MOCHA COCONUT

1 pint heavy cream
1 pint half & half
1 teaspoon pure vanilla extract
⅞ cup sugar
1 teaspoon coconut flavoring
2 ½ teaspoons unsweetened cocoa
6 ounces fresh brewed double strength coffee
½ cup flaked sweetened coconut toasted in a
300° degree oven for 6-8 minutes

Put the toasted coconut in the freezer. Add 2 coffee measures (4 level tablespoons) of ground coffee to 8 ounces of boiling water and stir. Let steep for 3 minutes and filter. Combine 6 ounces of the coffee and all of the other ingredients except the heavy cream and toasted coconut in a blender and run at highest speed for 30 seconds. Transfer the mixture to the freezing container and put in the freezer for 20 minutes.

Then, separately whip the heavy cream until set but not stiff, and the cream just barely falls off the beater blades. Add the whipped cream to the container and whip briefly to blend. Freeze as directed. When complete, remove the dasher or paddle, stir in the coconut with a spatula, and transfer the ice cream to a freezer container.

ORANGE BANANA

1 pint heavy cream
1 pint half & half
1 teaspoon pure vanilla extract
¾ cup sugar
1 teaspoon fine grated orange rind
4 ounces fresh squeezed orange juice
6 ounces banana, ripe but firm with brown spots on the skin but not on the fruit

Take 1 tablespoon of the sugar and the rind, and using a mortar and pestle, or with a custard cup or small glass and wooden spoon handle, mash and grind them together until the rind is further broken up and the sugar turns orange.

Put all of the ingredients except the heavy cream in a blender and blend at highest speed for 30 seconds. Transfer the mixture to the freezing container and put it in the freezer for 20 minutes.

Then, separately whip the heavy cream until set but not stiff and the cream just barely falls off the beater blades. Add the whipped cream to the container and whip briefly to blend. Freeze as directed.

PEACH

1 pint heavy cream
1 pint half & half
1 teaspoon pure vanilla extract
1 cup sugar
1 ½ fresh peaches, peeled, pitted and sliced
2 tablespoons Peach Brandy (optional)

Combine in a blender all of the ingredients except the heavy cream and blend at highest speed for 30 seconds. Transfer the mixture to the freezing container and put it in the freezer for 20 minutes.

Then, separately whip the heavy cream until set but not stiff and the cream just barely falls off the beater blades. Add the whipped cream to the container and whip briefly to blend. Freeze as directed.

Peaches have a fairly mild flavor and I recommend the brandy to boost the flavor a bit. You can add more of the fruit but that puts more water into your mixture. Of all the fruits peaches seem to suffer the most in a frozen or canned form. This recipe less the brandy is the same for nectarines.

CHOCOLATE HONEY

1 pint heavy cream
1 pint half & half
1 teaspoon pure vanilla extract
3 ounces sugar
3 ounces honey
2 ounces unsweetened cocoa

Put all of the ingredients except the heavy cream into a blender and run at highest speed for 30 seconds. Transfer the mixture to the freezing container and put it in the freezer for 20 minutes.

Then, separately whip the heavy cream until set but not stiff, and the cream just barely falls off the beater blades. Add the whipped cream to the container mix and whip briefly to blend. Freeze as directed.

GINGER

1 pint heavy cream
1 pint half & half
½ teaspoon pure vanilla extract
¾ cup sugar
1 teaspoon powdered ginger
2 teaspoons fine grated ginger

Put all of the ingredients except the heavy cream in a blender and run at highest speed for 30 seconds. Transfer the mixture to the freezing container and put it in the freezer for 20 minutes.

Then, separately whip the heavy cream until set but not stiff, and the cream just barely falls off the beater blades. Add the whipped cream to the container and whip briefly to blend. Freeze as directed.

This is a very refreshing flavor and the combination of the two gingers makes it warm and cool and sweet at the same time. This would be an ideal topping for fresh fruits, or a slice of cake.

COFFEE MAPLE WALNUT

1 pint heavy cream
1 pint half & half
1 teaspoon pure vanilla extract
2 tablespoons sugar
¾ cup pure maple syrup
½ teaspoon maple flavoring
¾ cup double strength fresh brewed coffee
½ cup chopped walnuts, picked over for pieces of shell

Put the walnuts in the freezer. Add 2 coffee measures (4 level tablespoons) of ground coffee to 8 ounces of boiling water and stir. Let steep for 3 minutes and filter.

In a blender put 6 ounces of the coffee and all of the ingredients except the heavy cream and walnuts and blend at the highest speed for 30 seconds. Transfer the mixture to the freezing container and put it in the freezer.

After 20 minutes, separately whip the heavy cream until set but not stiff, and the cream just barely falls off the beater blades. Add the whipped cream to the container and whip briefly to blend. Freeze as directed.

COCONUT LEMON

1 pint heavy cream
1 pint half & half
1 teaspoon pure vanilla extract
1 cup sugar
½ teaspoon (scant) coconut flavoring
1 teaspoon fine grated lemon rind, firmly
packed
2 ounces fresh squeezed lemon juice
½ cup flaked sweetened coconut toasted in a
300° oven for 6-8 minutes

Put the toasted coconut in the freezer. Take 1 tablespoon of the sugar and the rind, and using a mortar and pestle, or with a custard cup or small glass and wooden spoon handle, mash and grind them together until the rind is further broken up and the sugar turns yellow.

Put all of the ingredients except the heavy cream and coconut into a blender and blend at highest speed for 30 seconds. Transfer the mixture to the freezing container and put it in the freezer.

After 20 minutes, separately whip the heavy cream until set but not stiff, and the cream just barely falls off the beater blades. Add the whipped cream to the container and whip briefly to blend. Freeze as directed. When complete, remove the dasher or paddle, stir in the coconut with a spatula and transfer the ice cream to a freezer container.

SESAME MALT

1 pint heavy cream
1 pint half & half
1 teaspoon pure vanilla extract
¾ cup sugar
3 ounces sesame tahini (butter)
3 ounces malt powder

Combine all of the ingredients except the heavy cream in a blender and run at highest speed for 30 seconds. Transfer the mixture to the freezing container and put it in the freezer.

After 20 minutes, separately whip the heavy cream until set but not stiff, and the cream just barely falls off the beater blades. Add the whipped cream to the container and whip briefly to blend. Freeze as directed.

ANISE WITH ALMONDS

1 pint heavy cream
1 pint half & half
1 teaspoon pure vanilla extract
⅞ cup sugar
½ teaspoon anise extract
½ cup slivered almonds roasted in a 300° oven
for 10-15 minutes

Put the roasted almonds in the freezer. In a blender combine all of the ingredients except the heavy cream and nuts and blend at highest speed for 30 seconds. Transfer the mixture to the freezing container and put it in the freezer.

After 20 minutes, separately whip the heavy cream

until set but not stiff, and the cream just barely falls off the beater blades. Add the whipped cream to the container and whip briefly to blend. Freeze as directed. When complete, remove the dasher or paddle and stir in the almonds with a spatula, and transfer the ice cream to a freezer container.

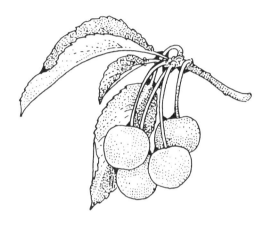

CHERRY

1 pint heavy cream
1 pint half & half
1 teaspoon pure vanilla extract
1 cup sugar
1 ½ cups pitted tart cherries, firm packed, fresh or canned and drained

In a blender put all of the ingredients except the heavy cream and blend at highest speed for 30 seconds. Transfer the mixture to the freezing container and put it in the freezer for 20 minutes.

Then, separately whip the heavy cream until set but not stiff, and the cream just barely falls off of the beater blades. Add the whipped cream to the container and whip briefly to blend. Freeze as directed.

CHOCOLATE COCONUT PEPPERMINT

1 pint heavy cream
1 pint half & half
1 teaspoon pure vanilla extract
⅞ cup sugar
½ teaspoon peppermint extract
1 teaspoon coconut flavoring
2 ounces unsweetened cocoa
½ cup flaked sweetened coconut, toasted for 6-8 minutes in a 300° oven

Put the toasted coconut in the freezer. In a blender combine all of the ingredients except the heavy cream and coconut and blend at high speed for 30 seconds. Transfer the mixture to the freezing container and put it in the freezer for 20 minutes.

Then, separately whip the heavy cream until set but not stiff, and the cream just barely falls off the beater blades. Add the whipped cream to the container and whip briefly to blend. Freeze as directed. When complete, remove the dasher or paddle, stir in the coconut with a spatula, and transfer the ice cream to a freezer container.

Here we have a flavor reminiscent of chocolate covered coconut peppermint patties. The trio of flavors makes a complex combination.

SESAME

1 pint heavy cream
1 pint half & half
1 teaspoon pure vanilla extract
⅞ cup sugar
3 ounces sesame tahini (butter)

Combine all of the ingredients except the heavy cream in a blender, and blend at highest speed for 30 seconds. Transfer the mixture to the freezing container and put it in the freezer.

After 20 minutes, separately whip the heavy cream until set but not stiff, and the cream just barely falls off the beater blades. Add the whipped cream to the container and whip briefly to blend. Freeze as directed.

This will remind you of halvah. The unique middle eastern sweet delight, which has a taste like nothing else. If you wish to make it more authentic, stir in some roasted, skinned, and unsalted pistachios.

HONEY SPEARMINT

1 pint heavy cream
1 pint half & half
½ teaspoon pure vanilla extract
½ teaspoon (scant) spearmint extract
½ cup honey
2 tablespoons sugar

In a blender put all of the ingredients, except the heavy cream, and blend at highest speed for 30 seconds. Transfer the mixture to the freezing container and put it in the freezer for 20 minutes.

Then, separately whip the heavy cream until set but not stiff, and the cream just barely falls off the beater blades. Add the whipped cream to the container mix and whip briefly to blend. Freeze as directed.

MOCHA ORANGE

1 pint heavy cream
1 pint half & half
1 teaspoon pure vanilla extract
1 cup sugar
1 teaspoon fine grated orange rind, firmly packed
6 ounces fresh brewed double strength coffee
2 ½ ounces unsweetened cocoa

Add 2 coffee measures (4 level tablespoons) of ground coffee to 8 ounces of boiling water and stir. Let steep for 3 minutes and filter. Take 1 tablespoon of the sugar and the rind, and using a mortar and pestle, or with a custard cup or small glass and wooden spoon handle, mash and grind them together until the rind is further broken up and the sugar turns orange.

In a blender add 6 ounces of the coffee and all of the other ingredients except the heavy cream and blend at highest speed for 30 seconds. Transfer the mixture to the freezing container and put it in the freezer for 20 minutes.

Then, separately whip the heavy cream until set but not stiff and the cream just barely falls off the beater blades. Add the whipped cream to the container and whip briefly to blend. Freeze as directed.

STRAWBERRY LIME

1 pint heavy cream
1 pint half & half
1 teaspoon pure vanilla extract
1 cup plus 1 ounce sugar
1 teaspoon fine grated lime rind firmly packed
1 ½ cups strawberries, fresh or whole
unsweetened

Take 1 tablespoon of the sugar and the rind, and using a mortar and pestle, or with a custard cup or small glass and wooden spoon handle, mash and grind them together until the rind is further broken up and the sugar turns green.

Put all of the ingredients except the heavy cream into a blender and blend at highest speed for 30 seconds. Transfer the mixture to the freezing container and put it in the freezer.

After 20 minutes, separately whip the heavy cream until set but not stiff and the cream just barely falls off the beater blades. Add the whipped cream to the container and whip briefly to blend. Freeze as directed.

This offers a nice and unexpected contrast to strawberry by itself which can be cloying.

PINEAPPLE

1 pint heavy cream
1 pint half & half
1 teaspoon pure vanilla extract
½ cup sugar
8 ounces frozen pineapple juice concentrate

Put all of the ingredients except the heavy cream into a blender and run at highest speed for 30 seconds. Transfer the mixture to the freezing container and put it in the freezer for 20 minutes.

Then, separately whip the heavy cream until set but not stiff and the cream just barely falls off the beater blades. Add the whipped cream to the container and whip briefly to blend.

Freeze as directed.

CHOCOLATE BANANA

1 pint heavy cream
1 pint half & half
1 teaspoon pure vanilla extract
¾ cup sugar
6 ounces banana, ripe but firm with brown spots on the skin but not on the fruit
1 teaspoon banana flavoring
2 ounces unsweetened cocoa

Put all of the ingredients except the heavy cream in a blender and blend at highest speed for 30 seconds. Transfer the mixture to the freezing container and put it in the freezer for 20 minutes.

Then, separately whip the heavy cream until set but not stiff, and the cream just barely falls off the beater blades. Add the whipped cream to the container mix and whip briefly to blend. Freeze as directed.

FIG ICE CREAM

1 pint heavy cream
1 pint half & half
1 ½ teaspoons pure vanilla extract
¼ cup sugar
⅔ cup water
⅔ cup dried black mission figs, stems removed,
quartered lengthwise and cut in half

Bring the water and figs in a sauce pan to a simmer and cook covered until the figs are very soft, in about 20 minutes.

In a blender combine all of the ingredients except the heavy cream and blend at highest speed for 30 seconds. Transfer the mixture to the freezing container and put it in the freezer for 20 minutes.

Then, separately whip the heavy cream until set but not stiff, and the cream just barely falls off of the beater blades. Add the whipped cream to the container and whip briefly to blend. Freeze as directed.

VANILLA

1 pint heavy cream
1 pint half & half
2 tablespoons pure vanilla extract
¾ cup sugar

Put everything except the heavy cream in a blender and run at highest speed for 30 seconds. Transfer the mixture to the freezing container and put it in the freezer for 20 minutes.

Then, separately whip the heavy cream until set but not stiff and the cream just barely falls off the beater blades. Add the whipped cream to the container and whip briefly to blend. Freeze as directed.

This mixture has more than the usual amount of vanilla. The most versatile of all flavors, and is especially full flavored.

HONEY & ALMOND BUTTER

1 pint heavy cream
1 pint half & half
1 teaspoon pure vanilla extract
2 tablespoons sugar
3 ounces honey
3 ounces almond butter

Put all of the ingredients except the heavy cream into a blender and run at highest speed for 30 seconds. Transfer the mixture to the freezing container and put it in the freezer for 20 minutes.

Then, separately whip the heavy cream until set but not stiff, and the cream just barely falls off the beater blades. Add the whipped cream to the container mix and whip briefly to blend. Freeze as directed.

The use of almond butter instead of almond flavoring is a great improvement. The latter is very harsh and tastes like a chemical, which it is.

CHOCOLATE LEMON

1 pint heavy cream
1 pint half & half
1 teaspoon pure vanilla extract
1 cup sugar
2 ounces unsweetened cocoa
1 ½ teaspoons fine grated lemon rind, firmly packed

Take 1 tablespoon of the sugar and the rind, and using a mortar and pestle, or with a custard cup or small glass and wooden spoon handle, mash and grind them together until the rind is further broken up and the sugar turns yellow.

Put all of the ingredients except the heavy cream into a blender and run at highest speed for 30 seconds. Transfer the mixture to the freezing container and put it in the freezer.

After 20 minutes, separately whip the heavy cream until set but not stiff, and the cream just barely falls off the beater blades. Add the whipped cream to the container and whip briefly to blend. Freeze as directed.

After orange chocolate, lemon chocolate seemed a natural, but I think, not lime.

APPLE

1 pint heavy cream
1 pint half & half
½ teaspoon pure vanilla extract
¾ cup sugar
1 cup Macintosh apples, peeled and sliced

71

Combine all of the ingredients, except the heavy cream in a blender and blend at highest speed for 30 seconds. Transfer the mixture to the freezing container and put it in the freezer.

After 20 minutes, separately whip the heavy cream until set but not stiff, and the cream just barely falls off the beater blades. Add the whipped cream to the container and whip briefly to blend. Freeze as directed.

Most other apples will work as well, but Macs are my favorite and this tastes just as fresh as the apple itself. How utterly different it is from the applesauce flavor I made earlier.

CHOCOLATE RUM WITH PECANS

1 pint heavy cream
1 pint half & half
1 teaspoon pure vanilla extract
7/8 cup sugar
3 ounces unsweetened cocoa
2 tablespoons dark rum
1 teaspoon rum flavoring
3/4 cup pecan halves, roasted at 275° for 15 minutes

Put the roasted pecans in the freezer. In a blender add all of the other ingredients except the heavy cream and pecans, and blend at highest speed for 30 seconds. Transfer the mixture to the freezing container and put the container in the freezer for 20 minutes.

Then, separately whip the heavy cream until set but not stiff, and the cream just barely falls off the beater blades. Add the whipped cream to the container and whip briefly to blend. Freeze as directed. When complete, remove the dasher or paddle, stir in the pecans with a spatula, and transfer the ice cream to a freezer container.

PISTACHIO

1 pint heavy cream
1 pint half & half
1 ½ teaspoons pure vanilla extract
1 cup and 1 ounce sugar
¼ teaspoon almond flavoring
1 tablespoon dark rum
½ cup pistachios, unsalted, shelled and skinned, and roasted for 15 minutes in a 300° oven

Put the roasted pistachios in the freezer. Add to a blender all of the ingredients except the heavy cream and nuts, and blend at highest speed for 30 seconds. Transfer the mixture to the freezing container and put it in the freezer for 20 minutes.

Then, separately whip the heavy cream until set but not stiff, and the cream just barely falls off the beater blades. Add the whipped cream to the container and whip briefly to blend. Freeze as directed. When complete, remove the dasher or paddle and stir in the pistachios with a spatula and transfer the ice cream to a freezer container.

MOCHA SESAME

1 pint heavy cream
1 pint half & half
1 teaspoon pure vanilla extract
1 cup sugar
2 ounces unsweetened cocoa
6 ounces fresh brewed double strength coffee
3 ounces sesame tahini (butter)

Add 2 coffee measure s (4 level tablespoons) of ground coffee to 8 ounces of boiling water and stir. Let the coffee steep for 3 minutes and filter.

In a blender, combine 6 ounces of the coffee and all of the ingredients except the heavy cream, and blend at highest speed for 30 seconds. Transfer the mixture to the freezing container and put it in the freezer for 20 minutes.

Then, separately whip the heavy cream until set but not stiff, and the cream just barely falls off the beater blades. Add the whipped cream to the container mix and whip briefly to blend. Freeze as directed.

CHOCOLATE PEANUT BUTTER

1 pint heavy cream
1 pint half & half
1 teaspoon pure vanilla extract
⅞ cup sugar
2 ounces unsweetened cocoa
3 ounces non-homogenized peanut butter

Put all of the ingredients except the heavy cream in a blender, and run at highest speed for 30 seconds. Transfer the mixture to the freezing container and put it in the freezer.

After 20 minutes, separately whip the heavy cream until set but not stiff and the cream just barely falls off the beater blades. Add the whipped cream to the container and whip briefly to blend. Freeze as directed.

GINGER LIME

1 pint heavy cream
1 pint half & half
1 teaspoon pure vanilla extract
⅞ cup sugar
¼ teaspoon fine grated lime rind, firmly packed
2 tablespoons freeze squeezed lime juice
2 ½ teaspoons fine grated ginger

Take 1 tablespoon of the sugar and the rind, and using a mortar and pestle, or with a custard cup or small glass and wooden spoon handle, mash and grind them together until the rind is further broken up and the sugar turns green.

Put all of the ingredients except the heavy cream into a blender, and blend at highest speed for 30 seconds. Transfer the mixture to the freezing container and put it in the freezer.

After 20 minutes, separately whip the heavy cream until set but not stiff, and the cream just barely falls off the beater blades. Add the whipped cream to the container and whip briefly to blend. Freeze as directed.

This is a robust combination. Each flavor wants to take precedence. You decide which wins.

RASPBERRY PEPPERMINT

1 pint heavy cream
1 pint half & half
1 teaspoon pure vanilla extract
1 cup sugar
½ teaspoon peppermint extract
1 ½ cups raspberries, fresh, or whole
unsweetened frozen

Put all of the ingredients except the heavy cream into a blender and run at highest speed for 30 seconds. Transfer the mixture to the freezing container and put it in the freezer.

After 20 minutes, separately whip the heavy cream until set but not stiff, and the cream just barely falls off the beater blades. Add the whipped cream to the container and whip briefly to mix. Freeze as directed.

This is an unexpected combination but people really like it.

COCONUT

1 pint heavy cream
1 pint half & half
1 teaspoon pure vanilla extract
¾ cup sugar
½ teaspoon coconut flavoring
½ cup flaked sweetened coconut toasted in a
300° oven for 6 - 8 minutes

Put the toasted coconut in the freezer. Add all of the ingredients, except the heavy cream and coconut to a blender and blend at highest speed for 30 seconds. Transfer the mixture to the freezing container and put it in the freezer for 20 minutes.

Then, separately whip the heavy cream until set but not stiff, and the cream just barely falls off the beater blades. Add the whipped cream to the container and whip briefly to blend. Freeze as directed. When complete, remove the dasher or paddle, stir in the coconut with a spatula, and transfer the ice cream to a freezer container.

CHOCOLATE ALMOND BUTTER

1 pint heavy cream
1 pint half & half
1 teaspoon pure vanilla extract
¾ cup sugar
2 ounces unsweetened cocoa
4 ounces well stirred almond butter

In a blender combine all of the ingredients except the heavy cream and blend at highest speed for 30 seconds. Transfer the mixture to the freezing container and put it in the freezer for 20 minutes.

Then, separately whip the heavy cream until set but not stiff, and the cream just barely falls off the beater blades. Add the whipped cream to the container and whip briefly to blend. Freeze as directed.

These are two of the richest and deepest flavors and they go very well together.

ALLSPICE

1 pint heavy cream
1 pint half & half
2 teaspoons pure vanilla extract
¾ cup sugar
½ teaspoon all spice powder, fresh ground from whole berries

Grind the berries with a mortar and pestle or an electric grinder to a fine powder. The powder you buy has already lost the fresh aroma that the berries still have and the difference is quite noticeable.

Combine all of the ingredients except the heavy cream in a blender and blend at highest speed for 30 seconds. Transfer the mixture to the freezing container and put it in the freezer.

After 20 minutes, separately whip the heavy cream until set but not stiff, and the cream just barely falls off

the beater blades. Add the whipped cream to the container and whip briefly to blend. Freeze as directed.

I also made ice cream this way using Szechuan peppercorns and star anise and surprisingly, the flavor was almost identical, but good in all three cases.

HONEY ORANGE

1 pint heavy cream
1 pint half & half
½ teaspoon pure vanilla extract
2 tablespoons sugar
½ cup honey
1 ½ teaspoons fine grated orange rind, firmly packed
2 ounces fresh squeezed orange juice

Take 1 tablespoon of the sugar and the orange rind, and using a mortar and pestle, or with a custard cup or small glass and wooden spoon handle, mash and grind them together until the rind is further broken up and the sugar turns orange.

Put all of the ingredients, except the heavy cream in the blender and blend at highest speed for 30 seconds. Transfer the mixture to the freezing container and put it in the freezer for 20 minutes.

Then, separately whip the heavy cream until set but not stiff, and the cream just barely falls off the beater blades. Add the whipped cream to the container mix, and whip briefly to blend. Freeze as directed.

VANILLA MALT

1 pint heavy cream
1 pint half & half
1 tablespoon pure vanilla extract
¾ cup sugar
2 ounces malt powder

Put all of the ingredients except the heavy cream in a blender and blend at highest speed for 30 seconds. Transfer the mixture to the freezing container and put it in the freezer.

After 20 minutes, separately whip the heavy cream until set but not stiff, and the cream just barely falls off the beater blades. Add the whipped cream to the container and whip briefly to blend. Freeze as directed.

PINEAPPLE PEACH

1 pint heavy cream
1 pint half & half
1 teaspoon pure vanilla extract
5 ounces sugar
1 ½ cups fresh peaches, peeled and sliced
4 ounces frozen pineapple juice concentrate

Put all of the ingredients except the heavy cream into a blender and blend at highest speed for 30 seconds. Transfer the mixture to the freezing container and put it in the freezer.

After 20 minutes, separately whip the heavy cream until set but not stiff and the cream just barely falls off the beater blades. Add the whipped cream to the container and whip briefly to blend. Freeze as directed.

BLUEBERRY

1 pint heavy cream
1 pint half & half
1 teaspoon pure vanilla extract
1 cup sugar
1 ½ cups blueberries, fresh or whole
unsweetened frozen

Put the berries in a saucepan on low heat and stir and mash them until the berries are cooked to a pulp (in 5 to 10 minutes). Strain the berries through a sieve and use a wooden spoon to force the pulp through the sieve. Be sure to scrape in any excess pulp from the outside of the strainer. Discard the skins. In the blender add all the other ingredients except the heavy cream and blend at highest speed for 30 seconds. Transfer the mixture to the freezing container and put it in the freezer for 20 minutes.

Then, separately whip the heavy cream until set but not stiff and the cream just barely falls off the beater blades. Add the whipped cream to the container and whip briefly to blend. Freeze as directed.

Before I thought of cooking the blueberries, I simply put them in a blender. But the pulp is a nondescript grayish color, the skin bits looked black, and the color was unappetizing. But this process releases the color and flavor which is just under the skin like grapes. This looks and tastes as it should.

CHOCOLATE CHILI WITH PINE NUTS

1 pint heavy cream
1 pint half & half
1 teaspoon pure vanilla extract
⅞ cup sugar
1 ½ teaspoons chili powder
3 ounces unsweetened cocoa
3 ounces pine nuts, toasted in a 275° oven for 6-10 minutes

Put the toasted pine nuts in the freezer. Combine all of the ingredients, except the heavy cream and pine nuts in a blender, and blend at highest speed for 30 seconds. Transfer the mixture to the freezing container and put it in the freezer for 20 minutes.

Then separately whip the heavy cream until set but not stiff, and the cream just barely falls off the beater blades. Add the whipped cream to the container and whip briefly to blend. Freeze as directed. When complete, remove the dasher or paddle and stir in the pine nuts with a spatula and transfer the ice cream to a freezer container.

For lovers of chocolate and chili this will appeal. Perhaps at the end of a Tex-Mex meal.

PEPPERMINT

1 pint heavy cream
1 pint half & half
1 teaspoon pure vanilla extract
¾ cup sugar
1 teaspoon peppermint extract

Put all of the ingredients except the heavy cream

in a blender and blend at highest speed for 30 seconds. Transfer the mixture to the freezing container and put it in the freezer.

After 20 minutes, separately whip the heavy cream until set but not stiff, and the cream just barely falls off the beater blades. Add the whipped cream to the container and whip briefly to blend. Freeze as directed.
No one ever mistakes this flavor and it would be fine over fresh fruit.

ORANGE CINNAMON

1 pint heavy cream
1 pint half & half
1 teaspoon pure vanilla extract
¾ cup sugar
¼ teaspoon cinnamon powder
1 teaspoon fine grated orange rind
4 ounces fresh squeezed orange juice

Take 1 tablespoon of the sugar and the rind, and using a mortar and pestle, or with a custard cup or small glass and wooden spoon handle, mash and grind them together until the rind is further broken up and the sugar turns orange.

Put all of the ingredients except the heavy cream in a blender and blend at highest speed for 30 seconds. Transfer the mixture to the freezing container and put it in the freezer. After 20 minutes, separately whip the heavy cream until set but not stiff, and the cream just barely falls off the beater blades. Add the whipped cream to the container and whip briefly to blend. Freeze as directed.

These are two great flavors mostly had around breakfast time, but not usually combined in the same dish.

LEMON GINGER

1 pint heavy cream
1 pint half & half
1 teaspoon pure vanilla extract
1 ¼ cups sugar
1 ½ teaspoons fine grated ginger
1 teaspoon fine grated lemon rind, firmly
packed
3 ounces fresh squeezed lemon juice

Take 1 tablespoon of the sugar and the rind, and using a mortar and pestle, or with a custard cup or small glass and wooden spoon handle, mash and grind them together until the rind is further broken up and the sugar turns yellow.

Put all of the ingredients into a blender and blend at highest speed for 30 seconds. Transfer the mixture to the freezing container and put it in the freezer.

After 20 minutes, separately whip the heavy cream until set but not stiff, and the cream just barely falls off the beater blades. Add the whipped cream to the container and whip briefly to blend. Freeze as directed.

COFFEE MALT WITH ROASTED PECANS

1 pint heavy cream
1 pint half & half
1 teaspoon pure vanilla extract
¾ cup sugar
3 ounces malt powder
6 ounces fresh brewed double strength coffee
¾ cup pecan halves roasted at 275° for 15
minutes

Put the roasted pecans in the freezer. Add 2 coffee measures (4 level tablespoons) of ground coffee to 8 ounces of boiling water and stir. Let the coffee steep for 3 minutes and filter.

In a blender add 6 ounces of the coffee, the half & half, sugar, malt, and vanilla, and blend at highest speed for 30 seconds. Transfer the mixture to the freezing container and put it in the freezer for 20 minutes.

Then, separately whip the heavy cream until set but not stiff and the cream just barely falls off the beater blades. Add the whipped cream to the container mix and whip briefly to blend. Freeze as directed. When complete, remove the dasher or paddle and stir in the pecans with a spatula, and transfer the ice cream to a freezer container.

PLUM

1 pint heavy cream
1 pint half & half
½ teaspoon pure vanilla extract
¾ cup sugar
1 ½ cups peeled and pitted fresh plums

Put all of the ingredients except the heavy cream into a blender and run at the highest speed for 30 seconds. Transfer the mixture to the freezing container and put it in the freezer.

After 20 minutes, separately whip the heavy cream until set but not stiff, and the cream just barely falls off the beater blades. Add the whipped cream to the container and whip briefly to blend. Freeze as directed.

CHOCOLATE MOLASSES

1 pint heavy cream
1 pint half & half
1 ½ teaspoons pure vanilla extract
¾ cup sugar
2 ounces unsulphured molasses
2 ounces unsweetened cocoa

In a blender, add all of the ingredients except the heavy cream and blend at highest speed for 30 seconds. Transfer the mixture to the freezing container and put it in the freezer for 20 minutes.

Then, separately whip the heavy cream until set but not stiff, and the cream just barely falls off the beater blades. Add the whipped cream to the container and whip briefly to blend. Freeze as directed.

PINE NUT

1 pint heavy cream
1 pint half & half
½ teaspoon pure vanilla extract
¾ cup sugar
½ cup pine nuts, toasted in a 275° oven for 6-10 minutes

Add the cooled nuts and all of the other ingredients except the heavy cream to a blender and blend at highest speed for 30 seconds. Transfer the mixture to the freezing container and put in the freezer.

After 20 minutes, separately whip the heavy cream until set but not stiff, and the cream just barely falls off the beater blades. Add the whipped cream to the container and whip briefly to blend.

The nuts should be lightly toasted, and are ready when they just turn color and become very lightly tan. They will quickly become dark and harsh tasting if over toasted.

COFFEE COCONUT

1 pint heavy cream
1 pint half & half
½ teaspoon pure vanilla extract
⅞ cup sugar
½ teaspoon coconut flavoring
¾ cup double strength fresh brewed coffee
½ cup flaked sweetened coconut, toasted in a 300° oven for 6-8 minutes

Put the toasted coconut in the freezer. Add 2 coffee measures (4 level tablespoons) of ground coffee to 8 ounces boiling water and stir. Let steep 3 minutes and filter.

Put 6 ounces of the coffee and all of the other ingredients except the heavy cream in a blender and blend at the highest speed for 30 seconds. Transfer the mixture to the freezing container and put it in the freezer.

After 20 minutes, separately whip the heavy cream until set but not stiff, and the cream just barely falls off the beater blades. Add the whipped cream to the container and whip briefly to blend. Freeze as directed. When complete, remove the dasher or paddle, stir in the coconut with a spatula, and transfer the ice cream to a freezer container.

87

PINEAPPLE MALT

1 pint heavy cream
1 pint half & half
1 teaspoon pure vanilla extract
¾ cup sugar
2 ounces malt powder
6 ounces frozen pineapple juice concentrate

In a blender put all of the ingredients except the heavy cream and blend at highest speed for 30 seconds. Transfer the mixture to the freezing container and put it in the freezer.

After 20 minutes, separately whip the heavy cream until set but not stiff, and the cream just barely falls off the beater blades. Add the whipped cream to the container and whip briefly to blend. Freeze as directed.

MOCHA MAPLE WALNUT

1 pint heavy cream
1 pint half & half
1 teaspoon pure vanilla extract
½ cup sugar
½ cup pure maple syrup
2 ounces unsweetened cocoa
6 ounces double strength fresh brewed coffee
½ teaspoon maple flavoring
½ cup walnuts

Put the walnuts in the freezer. Add 2 coffee measures (4 level tablespoons of ground coffee) to 8 ounces of boiling water and stir. Let steep 3 minutes and filter.

In a blender add 6 ounces of the coffee along with all of the other ingredients except the heavy cream and walnuts, and blend at highest speed for 30 seconds. Transfer the mixture to the freezing container and put it in the freezer.

After 20 minutes, separately whip the heavy cream until set but not stiff and the cream just barely falls off the beater blades. Add the whipped cream to the container and whip briefly to blend. Freeze as directed.

When complete, remove the dasher or paddle, stir in the walnuts with a spatula, and transfer the ice cream to a freezer container.

LIME

1 pint heavy cream
1 pint half & half
1 teaspoon pure vanilla extract
1 ¼ cups sugar
1 teaspoon fine grated lime rind, firmly packed
3 ounces fresh squeezed lime juice

Take 1 tablespoon of the sugar and the rind, and using a mortar and pestle, or with a custard cup or small glass and wooden spoon handle, mash and grind them together until the rind is further broken up and the sugar turns green.

Add all of the ingredients except the heavy cream to a blender and blend at the highest speed for 30 seconds. Transfer the mixture to the freezing container and put it in the freezer for 20 minutes.

Then, separately whip the heavy cream until set

but not stiff and the cream just barely falls off the beater blades. Add the whipped cream to the container and whip briefly to blend. Freeze as directed.

This is a very mellow and soothing flavor, quite unlike the lemon. I can't think of anything else where lime tastes as good. Perhaps only Key lime pie.

BLACK CURRANT

1 pint heavy cream
1 pint half & half
1 ½ teaspoons pure vanilla extract
⅞ cup sugar
¾ cup dried black (zante) currants
3 ounces water

Bring the water to a boil, add the currants, reduce the heat to a simmer, and cook covered for 3 minutes.

Put all of the ingredients except the heavy cream into a blender and run at highest speed for 30 seconds. Transfer the mixture to the freezing container and put it in the freezer for 20 minutes.

Then, separately whip the heavy cream until set but not stiff, and the cream just barely falls off the beater blades. Add the whipped cream to the container mix and whip to blend. Freeze as directed.

BANANA PINEAPPLE

1 pint heavy cream
1 pint half & half
1 teaspoon pure vanilla extract
¾ cup sugar

8 ounces frozen pineapple juice concentrate
3 ounces banana, ripe but firm with brown
spots on the skin but not on the fruit

Put all of the ingredients except the heavy cream into a blender and run it at highest speed for 30 seconds. Transfer the mixture to the freezing container and put it in the freezer.

After 20 minutes whip the heavy cream until set but not stiff, and the cream just barely falls off the beater blades. Add the whipped cream to the container and whip briefly to blend. Freeze as directed.

HONEY RUM

1 pint heavy cream
1 pint half & half
1 teaspoon pure vanilla extract
2 tablespoons sugar
½ cup honey
2 tablespoons dark rum
½ teaspoon rum extract

Put all of the ingredients except the heavy cream into a blender and run at the highest speed for 30 seconds. Transfer the mixture to the freezing container and put it into the freezer for 20 minutes.

Then, separately whip the heavy cream until set but not stiff, and the cream just barely falls off the beater blades. Add the whipped cream to the container mix and whip briefly to blend. Freeze as directed.

ORANGE ANISE WITH TOASTED PINE NUTS

1 pint heavy cream
1 pint half & half
½ teaspoon pure vanilla extract
¾ cup sugar
1 ½ teaspoons fine grated orange rind firmly packed
2 ounces fresh squeezed orange juice
3 ounces pine nuts roasted at 275° for 6-8 minutes

Put the roasted pine nuts in the freezer. Take 1 tablespoon of the sugar and the rind, and using a mortar and pestle, or with a custard cup or small glass and wooden spoon handle, mash and grind them together until the rind is further broken up and the sugar turns orange.

Put all of the ingredients except the heavy cream and pine nuts in a blender and blend at highest speed for 30 seconds. Transfer the mixture to the freezing container and put it in the freezer for 20 minutes.

Then, separately whip the heavy cream until set but not stiff, and the cream just barely falls off the beater blades. Add the whipped cream to the container mix, and whip briefly to blend. Freeze as directed.

When complete, remove the dasher or paddle and stir in the pine nuts with a spatula, and transfer the ice cream to a freezer container.

COFFEE MOLASSES

1 pint heavy cream
1 pint half & half
1 teaspoon pure vanilla extract
½ cup sugar
2 ounces unsulphured molasses
6 ounces double strength fresh brewed coffee

Add 2 coffee measures (4 level tablespoons) of ground coffee to 8 ounces of boiling water and stir. Let steep for 3 minutes and filter.

In a blender add 6 ounces of the coffee and all of the other ingredients except the heavy cream, and blend at highest speed for 30 seconds. Transfer the mixture to the freezing container and put it in the freezer for 20 minutes.

Then, separately whip the heavy cream until set but not stiff, and the cream just barely falls off the beater blades. Add the whipped cream to the container mix and whip briefly to blend. Freeze as directed.

MAPLE MALT WITH WALNUTS

1 pint heavy cream
1 pint half & half
1 teaspoon pure vanilla extract
2 ounces sugar
½ cup pure maple syrup
½ teaspoon maple flavoring
2 ounces malt powder
½ cup walnuts, picked over for shell parts

Put the walnuts in the freezer. In a blender combine all of the ingredients except the heavy cream and walnuts, and blend at highest speed for 30 seconds.

Transfer the mixture to the freezing container and put it in the freezer.

After 20 minutes, separately whip the heavy cream until set but not stiff, and the cream just barely falls off the beater blades. Add the whipped cream to the container and whip briefly to blend. Freeze as directed. When complete, remove the dasher or paddle and stir in the walnuts with a spatula, and transfer the ice cream to a freezer container.

BANANA

1 pint heavy cream
1 pint half & half
1 ½ teaspoons pure vanilla extract
¾ cup sugar
6 ounces banana, ripe but firm with brown spots on the skin but not on the fruit

Put all of the ingredients except the heavy cream in a blender and run at highest speed for 30 seconds. Transfer the mixture to the freezing container and put it in the freezer for 20 minutes.

Then, separately whip the heavy cream until set but not stiff and the cream just barely falls off the beater blades. Add the whipped cream to the container and whip briefly to blend. Freeze as directed.

GINGER PINEAPPLE

1 pint heavy cream
1 pint half & half
½ teaspoon pure vanilla extract
¾ cup sugar
¾ teaspoon fine grated ginger
6 ounces frozen pineapple juice concentrate

Put all of the ingredients except the heavy cream into a blender and blend at highest speed for 30 seconds. Transfer the mixture to the freezing container and put it in the freezer.

After 20 minutes, separately whip the heavy cream until set but not stiff, and the cream just barely falls off the beater blades. Add the whipped cream to the container and whip briefly to blend. Freeze as directed.

ORANGE MOLASSES

1 pint heavy cream
1 pint half & half
1 teaspoon pure vanilla extract
3 ounces sugar
2 ounces unsulphured molasses
1 ½ teaspoons fine grated orange rind, firmly packed **95**

Take 1 tablespoon of the sugar and the rind, and using a mortar and pestle, or with a custard cup or small glass and wooden spoon handle, mash and grind them together until the rind is further broken up and the sugar turns orange.

Put all of the ingredients except the heavy cream into a blender and blend at highest speed for 30 seconds. Transfer the mixture to the freezing container and put it in the freezer.

After 20 minutes, separately whip the heavy cream until set but not stiff, and the cream just barely falls off the beater blades. Add the whipped cream to the container and whip briefly to blend. Freeze as directed.

RASPBERRY CHOCOLATE

1 pint heavy cream
1 pint half & half
1 teaspoon pure vanilla extract
1 ¼ cups sugar
2 ounces unsweetened cocoa
1 ½ cups raspberries, fresh or whole, frozen unsweetened

Put all of the ingredients except the heavy cream into a blender and blend at highest speed for 30 seconds. Transfer the mixture to freezing container, and put it in the freezer.

After 20 minutes, separately whip the heavy cream until set but not stiff, and the cream just barely falls off the beater blades. Add the whipped cream to the container and whip briefly to blend. Freeze as directed.

The memory of a raspberry filled chocolate bar brought this combination to mind, and these two rich and robust flavors go very well together. If you are using fresh raspberries which are sweeter, lessen the amount of sugar by 1 ounce.

SPEARMINT

1 pint heavy cream
1 pint half & half
1 teaspoon pure vanilla extract
¾ cup sugar
1 teaspoon spearmint extract

Put all of the ingredients except the heavy cream in a blender and blend at highest speed for 30 seconds. Transfer the mixture to the freezing container and put it in the freezer.

After 20 minutes, separately whip the heavy cream until set but not stiff, and the cream just barely falls off the beater blades. Add the whipped cream to the container and whip briefly to blend. Freeze as directed.

This is a most refreshing flavor. Try it over fruit.

PEACH COCONUT

1 pint heavy cream
1 pint half & half
1 teaspoon pure vanilla extract
1 cup sugar
1 ½ cups fresh peaches, peeled and sliced
½ teaspoon (scant) coconut flavoring
½ cup flaked sweetened coconut, roasted in a
300° oven for 6-8 minutes

Put the toasted coconut in the freezer. Combine all of the ingredients except the heavy cream and coconut in a blender, and run at the highest speed for 30 seconds. Transfer the mixture to the freezing container and put it in the freezer.

After 20 minutes, whip the heavy cream until set but not stiff, and the cream just barely falls off the beater blades. Add the whipped cream to the container and whip briefly to blend. Freeze as directed. When complete, remove the dasher or paddle, stir in the coconut with a spatula and transfer the ice cream to a freezer container.

RUM PINEAPPLE

1 pint heavy cream
1 pint half & half
1 teaspoon pure vanilla extract
¾ cup sugar
1 teaspoon rum flavoring
8 ounces frozen pineapple juice concentrate

Add all of the ingredients except the heavy cream to a blender and blend at highest speed for 30 seconds. Transfer the mixture to the freezing container and put it in the freezer.

After 20 minutes, separately whip the heavy cream until set but not stiff, and the cream just barely falls off the beater blades. Add the whipped cream to the container and whip briefly to blend. Freeze as directed.

This flavor more than any other evokes tropical and exotic places.

GRAPEFRUIT

1 pint heavy cream
1 pint half & half
½ teaspoon pure vanilla extract
⅞ cup sugar
6 ounces fresh squeezed grapefruit juice
1 ½ teaspoons fine grated grapefruit rind, firmly packed

Take 1 tablespoon of the sugar and the rind, and using a mortar and pestle, or with a custard cup or small glass and wooden spoon handle, mash and grind them together until the rind is further broken up and the sugar turns pale yellow.

Put all of the ingredients except the heavy cream into a blender and run at highest speed for 30 seconds. Transfer the mixture to the freezing container and put it in the freezer.

After 20 minutes, separately whip the heavy cream until set but not stiff, and the cream just barely falls off the beater blades. Add the whipped cream to the container and whip briefly to blend. Freeze as directed.

CHOCOLATE CLOVE

1 pint heavy cream
1 pint half & half
1 teaspoon pure vanilla extract
⅞ cup sugar
½ teaspoon powdered clove
3 ounces unsweetened cocoa

In a blender put all of the ingredients except the heavy cream and run at highest speed for 30 seconds. Transfer the mixture to the freezing container and put it in the freezer for 20 minutes.

Then, separately whip the heavy cream until set but not stiff, and cream just barely falls off the beater blades. Add the whipped cream to the container and whip briefly to blend. Freeze as directed.

This combines the two richest and darkest flavors of all to make a most unusual ice cream.

CASHEW BUTTER

1 pint heavy cream
1 pint half & half
1 teaspoon pure vanilla extract
⅞ cup sugar
3 ounces cashew butter, well stirred

Combine all of the ingredients except the heavy cream in a blender and run at highest speed for 30 seconds. Transfer the mixture to the freezing container and put it in the freezer.

After 20 minutes, separately whip the heavy cream until set but not stiff, and the cream just barely falls off the beater blades. Add the whipped cream to the container and whip briefly to blend. Freeze as directed.

Smooth and rich just like the roasted nuts. I couldn't think of anything else that might go with it.

PEPPERMINT PINEAPPLE

1 pint heavy cream
1 pint half & half
1 teaspoon pure vanilla extract
¾ cup sugar
½ teaspoon peppermint extract
6 ounces frozen pineapple juice concentrate

Put all of the ingredients except the heavy cream in a blender and run at highest speed for 30 seconds. Transfer the mixture to the freezing container, and put it in the freezer.

After 20 minutes, separately whip the heavy cream until set but not stiff, and the cream just barely falls off the beater blades. Add the whipped cream to the container and whip briefly to blend. Freeze as directed.

I want to say, "don't laugh"! I woke up one morning with this decidedly unusual combination running through my head, but it really works, and peppermint runs very low on my scale of favorite flavors.

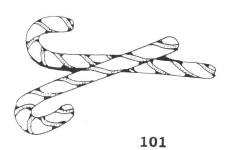

MOCHA MOLASSES WITH WALNUTS

1 pint heavy cream
1 pint half & half
1 teaspoon pure vanilla extract
5 ounces sugar
2 ounces unsweetened cocoa
6 ounces double strength fresh brewed coffee
2 ounces unsulphured molasses
½ cup walnut pieces, picked over to remove shell parts

Put the walnuts in the freezer. Add 2 coffee measures (4 level tablespoons) of ground coffee to 8 ounces of boiling water and stir. Let steep 3 minutes and filter.

In a blender combine 6 ounces of the coffee and all of the other ingredients except the heavy cream and walnuts and blend at highest speed for 30 seconds. Transfer the mixture to the freezing container and put it in the freezer for 20 minutes.

Then, separately whip the heavy cream until set but not stiff and the cream just barely falls off the beater blades. Add the whipped cream to the container and whip briefly to blend. Freeze as directed. When complete, remove the dasher or paddle and stir in the walnuts with a spatula and transfer the ice cream to a freezer container.

LEMON BANANA

1 pint heavy cream
1 pint half & half
½ teaspoon pure vanilla extract
⅞ cup sugar
1 teaspoon fine grated lemon rind
2 tablespoons fresh squeezed lemon juice
½ cup banana, ripe but firm with brown spots on the skin but not on the fruit

Take 1 tablespoon of the sugar and the rind and using a mortar and the pestle, or with a custard cup or small glass and wooden spoon handle, mash and grind them together until the rind is further broken up and the sugar turns yellow.

In a blender put all of the ingredients except the heavy cream and blend at highest speed for 30 seconds. Transfer the mixture to the freezing container and put it in the freezer for 20 minutes.

Then separately whip the heavy cream until set but not stiff and the cream just barely falls off the beater blades. Add the whipped cream to the container and whip briefly to blend. Freeze as directed.

PRUNE

1 pint heavy cream
1 pint half & half
1 ½ teaspoons pure vanilla extract
4 ounces sugar
1 cup cooked pitted prunes, firmly packed

Put all of the ingredients except the heavy cream

in a blender and blend at highest speed for 30 seconds. Transfer the mixture to the freezing container and put it in the freezer for 20 minutes.

Then separately whip the heavy cream until set but not stiff, and the cream just barely falls off the beater blades. Add the whipped cream to the container and whip briefly to blend.

CHOCOLATE MALT

1 pint heavy cream
1 pint half & half
1 teaspoon pure vanilla extract
⅞ cup sugar
2 ounces unsweetened cocoa
2 ounces malt powder

Put all of the ingredients except the heavy cream into a blender and blend at highest speed for 30 seconds. Transfer the mixture to the freezing container.

After 20 minutes, separately whip the heavy cream until set but not stiff, and the cream just barely falls off the beater blades. Add the whipped cream to the container and whip briefly to blend. Freeze as directed.

MAPLE WALNUT

1 pint heavy cream
1 pint half & half
1 ½ teaspoons pure vanilla extract
¼ cup sugar
¾ cup pure maple syrup
1 teaspoon maple flavoring
¾ cup walnut pieces, picked over for pieces of shell

Put the walnuts in the freezer. In a blender combine all of the ingredients except the heavy cream and walnuts and blend at highest speed for 30 seconds. Transfer the mixture to the freezing container and put it in the freezer for 20 minutes.

Then, separately whip the heavy cream until set but not stiff, and the cream just barely falls off the beater blades. Add the whipped cream to the container and whip briefly to blend. Freeze as directed. When complete, remove the dasher or paddle and stir in the walnuts with a spatula, and transfer the ice cream to a freezer container.

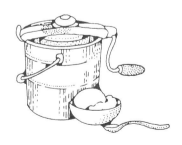

LEMON SPEARMINT

1 pint heavy cream
1 pint half & half
½ teaspoon pure vanilla extract
¾ cup sugar
2 teaspoons fine grated lemon rind
2 ounces fresh squeezed lemon juice
½ teaspoon spearmint extract

Take 1 tablespoon of the sugar and the rind, and using a mortar and pestle, or with a custard cup or small glass and wooden spoon handle, mash and grind them together, until the rind is further broken up and the sugar turns yellow.

Combine all of the ingredients except the heavy cream in a blender and run at highest speed for 30 seconds. Transfer the mixture to the freezing container and put it in the freezer for 20 minutes.

Transfer the mixture to the freezing container and put it in the freezer for 20 minutes.

Then, separately whip the heavy cream until set but not stiff, and the cream just barely falls off the beater blades. Add the whipped cream to the container and whip briefly to blend. Freeze as directed.

If you are using fresh strawberries, use only 1 cup of sugar. They are sweeter than commercially grown varieties.

CHOCOLATE PINEAPPLE

1 pint heavy cream
1 pint half & half
1 teaspoon pure vanilla extract
¾ cup sugar
2 ounces unsweetened cocoa
6 ounces frozen concentrated pineapple juice

Put all of the ingredients except the heavy cream in a blender and blend at highest speed for 30 seconds. Transfer the mixture to the freezing container and put it in the freezer for 30 seconds. Transfer the mixture to the freezing container and put it in the freezer for 20 minutes.

Then, separately whip the heavy cream until set but not stiff, and the cream just barely falls off the beater blades. Add the whipped cream to the container and whip briefly to blend. Freeze as directed.

This is a robust flavor and the tangy pineapple compliments the smooth and easy chocolate to make a marvelous combination.

RUM RAISIN

1 pint heavy cream
1 pint half & half
1 teaspoon pure vanilla extract
¾ cup sugar
3 ounces dark rum
¾ cup dark raisins

Combine the rum and raisins in a covered jar and let stand overnight. Shake occasionally.

In a blender strain in the excess rum and add all of the other ingredients except the heavy cream and raisins, and blend at highest speed for 30 seconds. Transfer the mixture to the serving container and put it in the freezer for 20 minutes. Also put the raisins in the freezer.

Then separately whip the heavy cream until set but not stiff and the cream just barely falls off the beater blades. Add the whipped cream to the container and whip briefly to blend. Freeze as directed. When complete, remove the dasher or paddle and stir in the raisins with a spatula and transfer the ice cream to a freezer container.

HONEY LIME

1 pint heavy cream
1 pint half & half
1 teaspoon pure vanilla extract
2 tablespoons sugar
3 ounces honey
½ teaspoon fine grated lime rind, firmly packed

Take 1 tablespoon of the sugar and the rind, and using a mortar and the pestle, or with a custard cup or small glass and wooden spoon handle, mash and grind them together until the rind is further broken up and the sugar turns green.

In a blender add all of the ingredients except the heavy cream and blend at highest speed for 30 seconds. Transfer the mixture to the freezing container and put it in the freezer for 20 minutes.

Then, separately whip the heavy cream until set but not stiff, and the cream just barely falls off the beater blades. Add the whipped cream to the container and whip briefly to blend. Freeze as directed.

ORANGE PEACH

1 pint heavy cream
1 pint half & half
½ teaspoon pure vanilla extract
¾ cup sugar
1 ½ cups fresh peeled sliced peaches
1 teaspoon fine grated orange rind, firmly packed

Take 1 tablespoon of the sugar and the rind, and using a mortar and pestle, or with a custard cup and wooden spoon handle, mash and grind them together until the rind is broken up and the sugar turns orange.

Put all of the ingredients except the heavy cream into a blender, and run at highest speed for 30 seconds. Transfer the mixture to the freezing container and put it in the freezer.

After 20 minutes, separately whip the heavy cream until set but not stiff, and the cream just barely falls off the beater blades. Add the whipped cream to the container and whip briefly to blend. Freeze as directed.

STRAWBERRY

1 pint heavy cream
1 pint half & half
1 ½ teaspoons pure vanilla extract
1 ¼ cups sugar
1 ½ cups strawberries, fresh or whole
unsweetened frozen

Add all of the ingredients except the heavy cream to a blender, and run at highest speed for 30 seconds.

PAPAYA

1 pint heavy cream
1 pint half & half
1 teaspoon pure vanilla extract
¾ cup sugar
1 ½ cups fresh papaya fruit

In a blender put all of the ingredients except the heavy cream, and blend at highest speed for 30 seconds. Transfer the mixture to the freezing container and put it in the freezer for 20 minutes.

Then, separately whip the heavy cream until set but not stiff, and the cream just barely falls off the beater blades. Add the whipped cream to the container and whip briefly to blend. Freeze as directed.

CHOCOLATE EGG NOG

1 pint heavy cream
1 pint half & half
2 teaspoons pure vanilla extract
⅞ cup sugar
2 ounces unsweetened cocoa

¼ teaspoon nutmeg
½ teaspoon (scant) rum flavoring

In a blender add all of the ingredients except the heavy cream and blend at highest speed for 30 seconds. Transfer the mixture to the freezing container and put it in the freezer for 20 minutes.

Then, separately whip the heavy cream until set but not stiff and the cream just barely falls off the beater blades. Add the whipped cream to the container mix and whip briefly to blend. Freeze as directed.

Then separately whip the heavy cream until set but not stiff, and the cream just barely falls off the beater blades. Add the whipped cream to the container and whip briefly to blend. Freeze as directed.

PEANUT BUTTER MOLASSES

1 pint heavy cream
1 pint half & half
1 teaspoon pure vanilla extract
3 ounces sugar
2 ounces unsulphured molasses
3 ounces non-homogenized peanut butter

In a blender combine all of the ingredients except the heavy cream and blend at highest speed for 30 seconds. Transfer the mixture to the freezing container and put in the freezer for 20 minutes.

Then, separately whip the heavy cream until set but not stiff, and the cream just barely falls off the beater blades. Add the whipped cream to the container and whip briefly to blend. Freeze as directed.

ALMOND BUTTER

1 pint heavy cream
½ pint half & half
½ pint regular milk
1 ½ teaspoons pure vanilla extract
¾ cup sugar
4 ounces almond butter, well stirred

Put all of the ingredients except the heavy cream in a blender and blend at highest speed for 30 seconds. Transfer the mixture to the freezing container and put it in the freezer.

After 20 minutes, separately whip the heavy cream until set but not stiff, and the cream just barely falls off the beater blades. Add the whipped cream to the container and whip briefly to blend. Freeze as directed.

The density of the almond butter makes it necessary to substitute milk to lower the cream content so that the texture will not be too heavy.

HONEY WITH PINE NUTS

1 pint heavy cream
1 pint half & half
1 ½ teaspoons pure vanilla extract
½ cup honey
3 ounces pine nuts toasted in a 275° oven for 6-10 minutes

Put the toasted pine nuts in the freezer. Add all of the ingredients except the heavy cream and pine nuts to a blender and run at highest speed for 30 seconds. Transfer the mixture to the freezing container and put it in the freezer for 20 minutes.

Then, separately whip the heavy cream until set but not stiff, and the cream just barely falls off the beater blades. Add the whipped cream to the container mix and whip briefly to blend. Freeze as directed. When complete, remove the dasher or paddle, stir in the nuts with a spatula, and transfer the ice cream to a freezer container.

MOCHA EGG NOG

1 pint heavy cream
1 pint half & half
1 teaspoon pure vanilla extract
1 cup sugar
½ teaspoon nutmeg
2 ounces unsweetened cocoa
½ teaspoon (scant) rum flavoring
6 ounces fresh brewed double strength coffee

Add 2 coffee measures (4 level tablespoons) of ground coffee to 8 ounces of boiling water and stir. Let the coffee steep for 3 minutes and filter.

In a blender add 6 ounces of the coffee, and all other ingredients except the heavy cream and blend at highest speed for 30 seconds. Transfer the mixture to the freezing container and put it in the freezer for 20 minutes.

Then, separately whip the heavy cream until set but not stiff, and the cream just barely falls off the beater blades. Add the whipped cream to the container mix and whip briefly to blend. Freeze as directed.

RASPBERRY LIME

1 pint heavy cream
1 pint half & half
1 teaspoon pure vanilla extract
⅞ cup sugar
½ teaspoon fine grated lime rind, firmly packed
1 ½ cups raspberries, fresh or whole
unsweetened frozen

Take 1 tablespoon of the sugar and the rind, and using a mortar and pestle, or with a custard cup or small glass and wooden spoon handle, mash and grind them together until the rind is further broken up and the sugar turns green.

Put all of the ingredients except the heavy cream into a blender and run at highest speed for 30 seconds. Transfer the mixture to the freezing container and put it in the freezer.

After 20 minutes, separately whip the heavy cream until set but not stiff and the cream just barely falls off the beater blades. Add the whipped cream to the container and whip briefly to blend. Freeze as directed.

Many years ago we used to get raspberry sodas with a splash of lime. It works well with ice cream too.

CHOCOLATE GINGER

1 pint heavy cream
1 pint half & half
1 teaspoon pure vanilla extract
¾ cup sugar
2 ounces unsweetened cocoa
3 teaspoons fine grated ginger

Put all of the ingredients except the heavy cream into a blender and run at highest speed for 30 seconds. Transfer the mixture to the freezing container and put it in the freezer for 20 minutes.

Then, separately whip the heavy cream until set but not stiff, and the cream just barely falls off the beater blades. Add the whipped cream to the container and whip briefly to blend. Freeze as directed.

TANGERINE

1 pint heavy cream
1 pint half & half
1 teaspoon pure vanilla extract
⅞ cup sugar
2 teaspoons fine grated tangerine rind
¾ cup fresh squeezed tangerine juice

Take 1 tablespoon of the sugar and the rind, and using a mortar and pestle, or with a custard cup or small glass and wooden spoon handle, mash and grind them together until the rind is further broken up and the sugar turns orange.

Add all of the ingredients, except the heavy cream to a blender and blend at highest speed for 30 seconds. Transfer the mixture to the freezing container and put it in the freezer for 25 minutes.

Then, separately whip the heavy cream until set but not stiff, and the cream just barely falls off the beater blades. Add the whipped cream to the mixture and whip briefly to blend. Freeze as directed.

This is a wonderful flavor, but unfortunately a seasonal one. Be sure to use tangerines whose skin (is rather loose), peels easily and whose rind when scratched has the characteristic odor of tangerines. Tangerine hybrids taste very different and usually peel with difficulty.

CHOCOLATE RUM RAISIN

1 pint heavy cream
1 pint half & half
1 teaspoon pure vanilla extract
⅞ cup sugar
3 ounces unsweetened cocoa
3 ounces dark rum
¾ cup dark raisins

Put the rum and raisins in a small covered jar and shake occasionally and leave overnight.

Strain the excess rum into a blender and put the raisins in the freezer. Add all of the other ingredients to the blender except the heavy cream and blend at highest speed for 30 seconds. Transfer the mixture to the freezing container and put it in the freezer for 20 minutes.

Then, separately whip the heavy cream until set but not stiff and the cream just barely falls off the beater blades. Add the whipped cream to the container and whip briefly to blend. Freeze as directed. When complete, remove the dasher or paddle and stir in the raisins with a spatula, and transfer the ice cream to a freezer container.

Plain rum raisin when it first came out was a favorite everywhere. I think you'll find that this goes it one better.

ROOT BEER

1 pint heavy cream
1 pint half & half
1 teaspoon pure vanilla extract
¾ cup sugar
1 teaspoon root beer concentrate

Put all of the ingredients except the heavy cream into a blender and blend at highest speed for 30 seconds. Transfer the mixture to the freezing container and put it in the freezer.

After 20 minutes, separately whip the heavy cream until set but not stiff, and the cream just barely falls off the beater blades. Add the whipped cream to the container and whip briefly to blend. Freeze as directed.

No surprises here, it tastes just as you'd expect. The kids will love it, perhaps with M & M's on top.

STRAWBERRY SPEARMINT

1 pint heavy cream
1 pint half & half
1 teaspoon pure vanilla extract
1 cup sugar
½ teaspoon spearmint extract
1 ½ cups strawberries, fresh, or whole frozen unsweetened

Put all of the ingredients except the heavy cream in a blender and run at highest speed for 30 seconds.

Transfer the mixture to the freezing container and put it in the freezer.

After 20 minutes, separately whip the heavy cream until set but not stiff, and the cream just barely falls off the beater blades. Add the whipped cream to the container and whip briefly to blend. Freeze as directed.

The idea for this one comes from recipes for desserts that feature whole strawberries and fresh mint leaves.

ORANGE GINGER

1 pint heavy cream
1 pint half & half
½ teaspoon pure vanilla extract
1 ¼ cups sugar
1 teaspoon fine grated ginger
1 teaspoon fine grated orange rind, firmly packed
¾ cup fresh squeezed orange juice

Take 1 tablespoon of the sugar and the rind, and using a mortar and pestle, or with a custard cup or small glass and wooden spoon handle, mash and grind them together until the rind is further broken up and the sugar turns orange.

Put all of the ingredients into a blender and run at highest speed for 30 seconds. Transfer the mixture to the freezing container and put it in the freezer.

After 20 minutes, separately whip the heavy cream until set but not stiff, and the cream just barely falls off the beater blades. Add the whipped cream to the container and whip briefly to blend. Freeze as directed.

SESAME MOLASSES

1 pint heavy cream
1 pint half & half
1 teaspoon pure vanilla extract
4 ounces sugar
2 ounces unsulphured molasses
3 ounces sesame tahini (butter)

Combine all of the ingredients except the heavy cream in a blender and blend at highest speed for 30 seconds. Transfer the mixture to the freezing container and put it in the freezer for 20 minutes.

Then, separately whip the heavy cream until set but not stiff, and the cream just barely falls off the beater blades. Add the whipped cream to the container and whip briefly to blend. Freeze as directed.

LEMON ANISE WITH ALMONDS

1 pint heavy cream
1 pint half & half
½ teaspoon pure vanilla extract
⅞ cup sugar
½ teaspoon anise extract
1 teaspoon fine grated lemon rind, firmly packed
3 ounces slivered almonds roasted in a 300° oven for 12-15 minutes

Put the roasted almonds in the freezer. Take 1 tablespoon of the sugar and the rind, and using a mortar and pestle, or with a custard cup or small glass and wooden spoon handle, mash and grind them together until the rind is further broken up and the sugar turns yellow.

In a blender combine all of the ingredients except the heavy cream and nuts and blend at the highest speed for 30 seconds. Transfer the mixture to the freezing container and put it in the freezer.

After 20 minutes, separately whip the heavy cream until set but not stiff, and cream just barely falls off the beater blades. Add the whipped cream to the container and whip briefly to blend. Freeze as directed. When complete, remove the dasher or paddle and stir in the almonds with a spatula and transfer the ice cream to a freezer container.

The idea for this flavor came from Italian biscotti cookies. Both are a delight.

CINNAMON COCONUT

1 pint heavy cream
1 pint half & half
1 teaspoon pure vanilla extract
¾ cup sugar
½ teaspoon (scant) coconut flavoring
¾ teaspoon cinnamon

Put all of the ingredients except the heavy cream into a blender and run at highest speed for 30 seconds. Transfer the mixture to the freezing container and put it in the freezer.

After 20 minutes, separately whip the heavy cream until set but not stiff, and the cream just barely falls off the beater blades. Add the whipped cream to the container and whip briefly to blend. Freeze as directed.

PEAR

1 pint heavy cream
1 pint half & half
½ teaspoon pure vanilla extract
¾ cup sugar
1 ½ cups ripe pears, peeled and sliced

Put all of the ingredients in a blender and blend at highest speed for 30 seconds. Transfer the mixture to the freezing container and put it in the freezer.

After 20 minutes, separately whip the heavy cream until set but not stiff, and the cream just barely falls off the beater blades. Add the whipped cream to the container and whip briefly to blend. Freeze as directed.

CHOCOLATE WITH ROASTED ALMONDS

1 pint heavy cream
1 pint half & half
1 teaspoon pure vanilla extract
1 cup sugar
2 ½ ounces unsweetened cocoa
¾ cup whole skinless almonds, roasted at 300°
for 15-20 minutes

Put the roasted almonds in the freezer.

Put all of the ingredients except the heavy cream and almonds in a blender and blend at highest speed for 30 seconds. Transfer the mixture to freezing container and put it in the freezer for 20 minutes.

Then, separately whip the heavy cream until set but not stiff, and the cream just barely falls off the beater blades. Add the whipped cream to the container and whip briefly to blend. Freeze as directed. When complete, remove the dasher or paddle and stir in the almonds with a spatula and transfer the ice cream to a freezer container.

EGG NOG

1 pint heavy cream
1 pint half & half
2 teaspoons pure vanilla extract
¼ teaspoon nutmeg
3 ounces dark rum (or ½ teaspoon rum flavoring and 1 tablespoon dark rum)

Put all of the ingredients in a blender except the heavy cream and blend at highest speed for 30 seconds. Transfer the mixture to the freezing container and put in the freezer for 20 minutes.

Then, separately whip the heavy cream until set but not stiff, and the cream just barely falls off the beater blades. Add the whipped cream to the container and whip briefly to blend. Freeze as directed.

If you didn't freeze this mixture as ice cream, it would be very similar to real egg nog, but here no eggs and much less liquor. You can also substitute 3 ounces of bourbon whiskey for the rum.

GINGER HONEY

1 pint heavy cream
1 pint half & half
1 teaspoon pure vanilla extract
3 ounces sugar
3 ounces honey
1 ½ teaspoons fine grated ginger

Put all of the ingredients except the heavy cream in a blender and blend at highest speed for 30 seconds. Transfer the mixture to the freezing container and put it in the freezer for 20 minutes.

Then, separately whip the heavy cream until set but not stiff, and the cream just barely falls off the beater blades. Add the whipped cream to the container and whip briefly to blend. Freeze as directed.

COCONUT LIME

1 pint heavy cream
1 pint half & half
1 teaspoon pure vanilla extract
⅞ cup sugar
½ teaspoon (scant) coconut flavoring
½ teaspoon fine grated lime rind, firmly packed
2 ounces fresh squeezed lime juice

Take 1 tablespoon of the sugar and the rind, and using a mortar and pestle, or with a custard cup or small glass and wooden spoon handle, mash and grind them together until the rind is further broken up and the sugar turns green.

Combine all of the ingredients except the heavy cream in a blender and run at highest speed for 30 seconds. Transfer the mixture to the freezing container and put it in the freezer.

After 20 minutes, separately whip the heavy cream until set but not stiff, and the cream just barely falls off the beater blades. Add the whipped cream to the container and whip briefly to blend. Freeze as directed.

VANILLA SPICE CREAM

1 pint heavy cream
1 pint half & half
2 teaspoons pure vanilla extract
⅞ cup sugar
1 teaspoon cinnamon
¼ teaspoon clove
¼ teaspoon nutmeg

Put all of the ingredients except the heavy cream into a blender and blend at highest speed for 30 seconds. Transfer the mixture to the freezing container and put it in the freezer.

After 20 minutes, separately whip the heavy cream until set but not stiff, and the cream just barely falls off the beater blades. Add the whipped cream to the container and whip briefly to blend. Freeze as directed.

CHOCOLATE SESAME

1 pint heavy cream
1 pint half & half
1 teaspoon pure vanilla extract
⅞ cup sugar
2 ounces unsweetened cocoa
4 ounces sesame butter (Tahini)

Combine all of the ingredients except the heavy cream in a blender and blend at highest speed for 30 seconds. Transfer the mixture to the freezing container and put it in the freezer for 20 minutes..

Then, separately whip the heavy cream until set but not stiff, and the cream just barely falls off the beater blades. Add the whipped cream to the container and whip briefly to blend. Freeze as directed.

If you like halvah, you will love this.

MALT

1 pint heavy cream
1 pint half & half
1 teaspoon pure vanilla extract
1 cup barley malt syrup

Put all of the ingredients except the heavy cream into a blender and run at highest speed for 30 seconds. Transfer the mixture to the freezing container and put it in the freezer.

After 20 minutes, separately whip the heavy cream until set but not stiff, and the cream just barely falls off the beater blades. Add the whipped cream to the container and whip briefly to blend. Freeze as directed.

This is the familiar taste of good old malt balls, and the taste is just as good here.

COFFEE CINNAMON

1 pint heavy cream
1 pint half & half
1 teaspoon pure vanilla extract
⅞ cup sugar
1 teaspoon cinnamon
8 ounces fresh brewed double strength coffee

Add 2 coffee measures (4 level tablespoons) to 1 ¼ cups of boiling water and stir. Let steep 3 minutes and filter.

In a blender combine 8 ounces of the coffee and all of the other ingredients except the heavy cream and blend at highest speed for 30 seconds. Transfer the mixture to the freezing container and put it in the freezer.

After 20 minutes, separately whip the heavy cream until set but not stiff, and the cream just barely falls off the beater blades. Add the whipped cream to the container and whip briefly to blend. Freeze as directed.

ORANGE RASPBERRY

1 pint heavy cream
1 pint half & half
1 teaspoon pure vanilla extract
1 ¼ cups sugar
1 teaspoon fine grated orange rind, firmly packed
1 ½ cups raspberries, fresh or whole unsweetened frozen

Take 1 tablespoon of the sugar and the rind, and using a mortar and pestle, or with a custard cup or small glass and wooden spoon handle, mash and grind them together until the rind is further broken up and the sugar turns orange.

Put all of the ingredients except the heavy cream in a blender and blend at the highest speed for 30 seconds. Transfer the mixture to the freezing container and put it in the freezer.

After 20 minutes, separately whip the heavy cream until set but not stiff, and the cream just barely falls off the beater blades. Add the whipped cream to the container and whip briefly to blend. Freeze as directed.

This is a happy creation for it contains the flavor of both my favorite juice and favorite berry. If you are using fresh raspberries which are sweeter than commercial, use only 1 cup of sugar.

COCONUT ALMOND BUTTER

1 pint heavy cream
1 pint half & half
1 teaspoon pure vanilla extract
¾ cup sugar
½ teaspoon (scant) coconut flavoring
3 ounces almond butter well stirred

Add all of the ingredients except the heavy cream to a blender and blend at highest speed for 30 seconds. Transfer the mixture to the freezing container and put it in the freezer.

After 20 minutes, separately whip the heavy cream until set but not stiff, and the cream just barely falls off the beater blades. Add the whipped cream to the container and whip briefly to blend. Freeze as directed.

LIME PINEAPPLE

1 pint heavy cream
1 pint half & half
1 teaspoon pure vanilla extract
¾ cup sugar
½ teaspoon (scant) fine grated lime rind, firmly packed
1 cup and 2 ounces frozen pineapple juice concentrate

Take 1 tablespoon of the sugar and the rind, and using a mortar and pestle, or with a custard cup or small glass and wooden spoon handle, mash and grind them together until the rind is further broken up and the sugar turns green.

Put all of the ingredients except the heavy cream into a blender and blend at highest speed for 30 seconds. Transfer the mixture to the freezing container and put it in the freezer for 20 minutes.

Then, separately whip the heavy cream until set but not stiff, and the cream just barely falls off the beater blades. Add the whipped cream to the container and whip briefly to blend.

Freeze as directed.

This is the last of the great trilogy of citrus fruit and pineapple based flavors, and it seems to be the most exotic. Perhaps because lime goes into far fewer foods than do the other two.

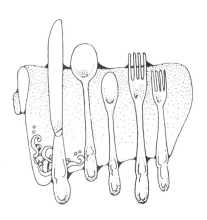

MOCHA MALT

1 pint heavy cream
1 pint half & half
1 teaspoon pure vanilla extract
⅞ cup sugar
2 ounces unsweetened cocoa
6 ounces double strength fresh brewed coffee
4 ounces malt powder

Add 2 coffee measures (4 level tablespoons) of ground coffee to 8 ounces of boiling water and stir. Let steep for 3 minutes and filter.

In a blender add 6 ounces of the coffee, and all of the other ingredients except the heavy cream and blend at highest speed for 30 seconds. Transfer the mixture to the freezing container and put it in the freezer for 20 minutes.

Then, separately whip the heavy cream until set but not stiff, and the cream just barely falls off the beater blades. Add the whipped cream to the container mix and whip briefly to blend. Freeze as directed.

HONEY SESAME

1 pint heavy cream
1 pint half & half
1 teaspoon pure vanilla extract
2 tablespoons sugar
3 ounces honey
3 ounces sesame butter (Tahini)

In a blender put all of the ingredients except the heavy cream, and blend at highest speed for 30 seconds. Transfer the mixture to the freezing container and put it in the freezer for 20 minutes.

Then, separately whip the heavy cream until set but not stiff, and the cream just barely falls off the beater blades. Add the whipped cream to the container and whip briefly to blend. Freeze as directed.

CHOCOLATE PEPPERMINT

1 pint heavy cream
1 pint half & half
½ teaspoon pure vanilla extract
⅞ cup sugar
1 teaspoon peppermint extract
2 ounces unsweetened cocoa

Put all of the ingredients except the heavy cream into a blender, and blend at highest speed for 30 seconds. Transfer the mixture to the freezing container and put it in the freezer.

After 20 minutes, separately whip the heavy cream until set but not stiff, and the cream just barely falls off the beater blades. Add the whipped cream to the container and whip briefly to blend.

Freeze as directed.

LEMON PECAN

1 pint heavy cream
1 pint half & half
½ teaspoon pure vanilla extract
¾ cup sugar
1 teaspoon fine grated lemon rind, firmly packed
¾ cup pecans, roasted at 275° for 15 minutes

Put all of the ingredients except the heavy cream into a blender, and blend at highest speed for 30 seconds. Transfer the mixture to the freezing container and put it in the freezer.

After 20 minutes, separately whip the heavy cream until set but not stiff, and the cream just barely falls off the beater blades. Add the whipped cream to the container and whip briefly to blend. Freeze as directed.

This combination was based on a lemon pecan cookie from my cookbook. This one is as good as that one.

AMBROSIA

1 pint heavy cream
1 pint half & half
½ teaspoon pure vanilla extract
1 cup sugar
1 teaspoon fine grated orange rind, firmly packed
1 ½ cups fresh peaches, peeled, pitted and sliced
2 tablespoons Galliano liquor (a must)

Take 1 tablespoon of the sugar and the rind, and using a mortar and pestle, or with a custard cup or small glass and wooden spoon handle, mash and grind them together until the rind is further broken up and the sugar turns orange.

Put all of the ingredients except the heavy cream into a blender and run at highest speed for 30 seconds.

Transfer the liquid to the freezing container and put it in the freezer.

After 20 minutes, separately whip the heavy cream until set but not stiff and the cream just barely falls off the beater blades. Add the whipped cream to the container and whip briefly to blend. Freeze as directed.

I saved this one for last, and it has the only title I could think of. It is worth the extra cost of the Galliano.

SOME ADDITIONAL UNTESTED FLAVORS

Chocolate Coconut
Chocolate Tangerine
Mocha Tangerine
Honey Tangerine
Peanut Butter Coconut
Chocolate Lemon Pineapple
Coconut Mango
Lemon Mango
Hazelnut
Pistachio Nut
Peppermint Lime
Chocolate Rum Pineapple
Chocolate Rum Banana
Coffee Butter Pecan
Honey Anise
Peach Lime
Chocolate Rum Anise with Pine Nuts
Rum Anise
Malt Pecan
Chocolate Banana Pineapple
Chocolate Orange Banana
Maple Peanut Butter
Ginger Rum
Walnut
Honey Maple

INDEX

All of the recipes are cross indexed so that each pair or trio of flavors are listed individually

Cinnamon Applesauce	45
Cinnamon Chocolate	50
Cinnamon Coconut	120
Cinnamon Coffee	127
Cinnamon Orange	83
Cinnamon Peach	25
Cinnamon Peppermint	56
Clove Chocolate	100
Coconut	76
Coconut Almond Butter	129
Coconut Banana	40
Coconut Chocolate Peppermint	64
Coconut Cinnamon	120
Coconut Coffee	87
Coconut Lemon	61
Coconut Lime	124
Coconut Mocha	56
Coconut Orange	47
Coconut Peach	98
Coconut Rum	28

Coffee Cinnamon	127
Coffee Coconut	87
Coffee Malt with Pecans	84
Coffee Maple Walnut	60
Coffee Molasses	93
Concord Grape	26
Cranberry	53
Egg Nog	122
Egg Nog Chocolate	110
Egg Nog Mocha	113
Fig	69
Ginger	59
Ginger Chocolate	114
Ginger Honey	123
Ginger Lemon	84
Ginger Lime	75
Ginger Orange	118
Ginger Molasses	48
Ginger Peach	31
Ginger Pineapple	95
Golden Raisin	55
Grapefruit	99
Honey with Pine Nuts	112
Honey Almond Butter	70
Honey Chocolate	59
Honey Chocolate Almond	43
Honey Ginger	123
Honey Lemon	37
Honey Lime	108
Honey Orange	79

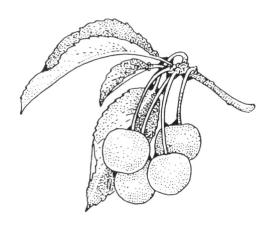

Orange with Pine Nuts	49
Orange with Anise with Pine Nuts	92
Orange Banana	57
Orange Chocolate	29
Orange Chocolate Pineapple	40
Orange Cinnamon	83
Orange Coconut	47
Orange Ginger	118
Orange Honey	79
Orange Mocha	66
Orange Molasses	95
Orange Peach	109
Orange Pineapple	27
Orange Raspberry	127
Orange Vanilla (Creamsicle)	35
Papaya	110
Peach	58
Peach Cinnamon	25
Peach Coconut	98
Peach Ginger	31
Peach Lemon	42
Peach Orange	109
Peach Peppermint	48
Peach Pineapple	80
Peanut Butter	36
Peanut Butter Banana	31

Peanut Butter Chocolate	74
Peanut Butter Malt	41
Peanut Butter Molasses	111
Peanut Butter Molasses Chocolate	54
Pear	121
Pecan	50
Pecan Lemon	133
Peppermint	82
Peppermint Chocolate	132
Peppermint Cinnamon	56
Peppermint Coconut Chocolate	64
Peppermint Molasses	34
Peppermint Peach	48
Peppermint Pineapple	101
Peppermint Raspberry	76
Pineapple	67
Pineapple Banana	89
Pineapple Chocolate	107
Pineapple Chocolate Orange	40

Pineapple Ginger	95
Pineapple Honey	51
Pineapple Lemon	53
Pineapple Lime	129
Pineapple Malt	88
Pineapple Orange	27
Pineapple Peach	80
Pineapple Peppermint	101
Pineapple Rum	98
Pine Nut	86
Pistachio	73
Plum	85
Prune	103
Raspberry	32
Raspberry Chocolate	96
Raspberry Lime	114
Raspberry Orange	127
Raspberry Peppermint	76
Root Beer	117
Rum Chocolate with Pecans	72
Rum Coconut	28
Rum Honey	90
Rum Mocha with Walnuts	52
Rum Pineapple	98
Rum Raisin	108
Rum Raisin Chocolate	116
Sesame Tahini	64
Sesame Tahini Chocolate	125
Sesame Tahini Honey	132
Sesame Tahini Malt	62
Sesame Tahini Mocha	73
Sesame Tahini Molasses	119

Spearmint	97
Spearmint Honey	65
Spearmint Lemon	106
Spearmint Strawberry	117
Strawberry	110
Strawberry Lime	67
Strawberry Spearmint	117
Tangerine	115
Vanilla	69
Vanilla Malt	80
Vanilla Orange (Creamsicle)	35
Vanilla Spice	125

Carol + Barbara

Jill

Debby C.

Sue + Rob

? Juliet

?

6-30-99
ordered

To Order Copies

• We Pay Shipping •

Please send me _____ copies:
          $9.95 each. (Make checks payable
to **QUIXOTE PRESS**.)

Name _____

Street _____

City _____ State _____ Zip _____

Hearts 'N Tummies Cookbook Co.
1854 - 345th Ave.
Wever, IA 52658
800-571-2665

- -

To Order Copies:

• We Pay Shipping •

Please send me _____ copies
          $9.95 each. (Make checks payable
to **QUIXOTE PRESS**.)

Name _____

Street _____

City _____ State _____ Zip _____

Hearts 'N Tummies Cookbook Co.
1854 - 345th Ave.
Wever, IA 52658
800-571-2665

Since you have enjoyed this book, perhaps you would be interested in some of these others from QUIXOTE PRESS.

ARKANSAS BOOKS

HOW TO TALK ARKANSAS
     by Bruce Carlson .... paperback $7.95
ARKANSAS' ROADKILL COOKBOOK
     by Bruce Carlson .... paperback $7.95
REVENGE OF ROADKILL
     by Bruce Carlson .... paperback $7.95
GHOSTS OF THE OZARKS
     by Bruce Carlson .... paperback $9.95
A FIELD GUIDE TO SMALL ARKANSAS FEMALES
     by Bruce Carlson .... paperback $9.95
LET'S US GO DOWN TO THE RIVER 'N...
     by various authors .... paperback $9.95
ARKANSAS' VANISHING OUTHOUSE
     by Bruce Carlson .... paperback $9.95
TALL TALES OF THE MISSISSIPPI RIVER
     by Dan Titus .... paperback $9.95
LOST & BURIED TREASURE OF THE MISSISSIPPI RIVER
     by Netha Bell & Gary Scholl .... paperback $9.95
TALES OF HACKETT'S CREEK
     by Dan Titus .... paperback $9.95
UNSOLVED MYSTERIES OF THE MISSISSIPPI RIVER
     by Netha Bell .... paperback $9.95
101 WAYS TO USE A DEAD RIVER FLY
     by Bruce Carlson .... paperback $7.95
VACANT LOT, SCHOOL YARD & BACK ALLEY GAMES
     by various authors .... paperback $9.95
HOW TO TALK MIDWESTERN
     by Robert Thomas .... paperback $7.95
ARKANSAS COOKIN'
     by Bruce Carlson .... (3x5) paperback $5.95

DAKOTA BOOKS

HOW TO TALK DAKOTA .... paperback $7.95
Some Pretty Tame, but Kinda Funny Stories About Early
DAKOTA LADIES-OF-THE-EVENING
     by Bruce Carlson .... paperback $9.95

SOUTH DAKOTA ROADKILL COOKBOOK
by Bruce Carlson .... paperback $7.95
REVENGE OF ROADKILL
by Bruce Carlson .... paperback $7.95
101 WAYS TO USE A DEAD RIVER FLY
by Bruce Carlson .... paperback $7.95
LET'S US GO DOWN TO THE RIVER 'N...
by various authors .... paperback $9.95
LOST & BURIED TREASURE OF THE MISSOURI RIVER
by Netha Bell .... paperback $9.95
MAKIN' DO IN SOUTH DAKOTA
by various authors .... paperback $9.95
GUNSHOOTIN', WHISKEY DRINKIN', GIRL CHASIN' STORIES
OUT OF THE OLD DAKOTAS
by Netha Bell .... paperback $9.95
THE DAKOTAS' VANISHING OUTHOUSE
by Bruce Carlson .... paperback $9.95
VACANT LOT, SCHOOL YARD & BACK ALLEY GAMES
by various authors .... paperback $9.95
HOW TO TALK MIDWESTERN
by Robert Thomas .... paperback $7.95
DAKOTA COOKIN'
by Bruce Carlson .... (3x5) paperback $5.95

ILLINOIS BOOKS

ILLINOIS COOKIN'
by Bruce Carlson .... (3x5) paperback $5.95
THE VANISHING OUTHOUSE OF ILLINOIS
by Bruce Carlson .... paperback $9.95
A FIELD GUIDE TO ILLINOIS' CRITTERS
by Bruce Carlson .... paperback $7.95
YOU KNOW YOU'RE IN ILLINOIS WHEN...
by Bruce Carlson .... paperback $7.95
Some Pretty Tame, but Kinda Funny Stories About Early
ILLINOIS LADIES-OF-THE-EVENING
by Bruce Carlson .... paperback $9.95
ILLINOIS' ROADKILL COOKBOOK
by Bruce Carlson .... paperback $7.95
101 WAYS TO USE A DEAD RIVER FLY
by Bruce Carlson .... paperback $7.95

HOW TO TALK ILLINOIS
    by Netha Bell .... paperback $7.95
TALL TALES OF THE MISSISSIPPI RIVER
    by Dan Titus .... paperback $9.95
TALES OF HACKETT'S CREEK
    by Dan Titus .... paperback $9.95
UNSOLVED MYSTERIES OF THE MISSISSIPPI
    by Netha Bell .... paperback $9.95
LOST & BURIED TREASURE OF THE MISSISSIPPI RIVER
    by Netha Bell & Gary Scholl .... paperback $9.95
STRANGE FOLKS ALONG THE MISSISSIPPI
    by Pat Wallace .... paperback $9.95
LET'S US GO DOWN TO THE RIVER 'N...
    by various authors .... paperback $9.95
MISSISSIPPI RIVER PO' FOLK
    by Pat Wallace .... paperback $9.95
GHOSTS OF THE MISSISSIPPI RIVER (from Keokuk to St. Louis)
    by Bruce Carlson .... paperback $9.95
GHOSTS OF THE MISSISSIPPI RIVER (from Dubuque to Keokuk)
    by Bruce Carlson .... paperback $9.95
MAKIN' DO IN ILLINOIS
    by various authors .... paperback $9.95
MY VERY FIRST
    by various authors .... paperback $9.95
VACANT LOT, SCHOOL YARD & BACK ALLEY GAMES
    by various authors .... paperback $9.95
HOW TO TALK MIDWESTERN
    by Robert Thomas .... paperback $7.95

INDIANA BOOKS

HOW TO TALK INDIANA .... paperback $7.95
INDIANA'S ROADKILL COOKBOOK
    by Bruce Carlson .... paperback $7.95
REVENGE OF ROADKILL
    by Bruce Carlson .... paperback $7.95
A FIELD GUIDE TO SMALL INDIANA FEMALES
    by Bruce Carlson .... paperback $9.95
GHOSTS OF THE OHIO RIVER (from Cincinnati to Louisville)
    by Bruce Carlson .... paperback $9.95
LET'S US GO DOWN TO THE RIVER 'N...
    by various authors .... paperback $9.95

101 WAYS TO USE A DEAD RIVER FLY
     by Bruce Carlson .... paperback $7.95
INDIANA'S VARNISHING OUTHOUSE
     by Bruce Carlson .... paperback $9.95
VACANT LOT, SCHOOL YARD & BACK ALLEY GAMES
     by various authors .... paperback $9.95
HOW TO TALK MIDWESTERN
     by Robert Thomas .... paperback $7.95

IOWA BOOKS

IOWA COOKIN'
     by Bruce Carlson .... (3x5) paperback $5.95
IOWA'S ROADKILL COOKBOOK
     By Bruce Carlson .... paperback $7.95
REVENGE OF ROADKILL
     by Bruce Carlson .... paperback $7.95
IOWA'S OLD SCHOOLHOUSES
     by Carole Turner Johnston .... paperback $9.95
GHOSTS OF THE AMANA COLONIES
     by Lori Erickson .... paperback $9.95
GHOSTS OF THE IOWA GREAT LAKES
     by Bruce Carlson .... paperback $9.95
GHOSTS OF THE MISSISSIPPI RIVER (from Dubuque to Keokuk)
     by Bruce Carlson .... paperback $9.95
GHOSTS OF THE MISSISSIPPI RIVER (from Minneapolis to Dubuque)
     by Bruce Carlson .... paperback $9.95
GHOSTS OF POLK COUNTY, IOWA
     by Tom Welch .... paperback $9.95
TALES OF HACKETT'S CREEK
     by Dan Titus .... paperback $9.95
ME 'N WESLEY (stories about the homemade toys that
  Iowa farm children made and played with around the turn of the century)
     by Bruce Carlson .... paperback $9.95
TALL TALES OF THE MISSISSIPPI RIVER
     by Dan Titus .... paperback $9.95
HOW TO TALK IOWA .... paperback $7.95
UNSOLVED MYSTERIES OF THE MISSISSIPPI
     by Netha Bell .... paperback $9.95
101 WAYS TO USE A DEAD RIVER FLY
     by Bruce Carlson .... paperback $7.95

LET'S US GO DOWN TO THE RIVER 'N...
      by various authors .... paperback $9.95

TRICKS WE PLAYED IN IOWA
      by various authors .... paperback $9.95

IOWA, THE LAND BETWEEN THE VOWELS
  (farm boy stories from the early 1900s)
      by Bruce Carlson .... paperback $9.95

LOST & BURIED TREASURE OF THE MISSISSIPPI RIVER
      by Netha Bell & Gary Scholl .... paperback $9.95

Some Pretty Tame, but Kinda Funny Stories About Early
IOWA LADIES-OF-THE-EVENING
      by Bruce Carlson .... paperback $9.95

THE VANISHING OUTHOUSE OF IOWA
      by Bruce Carlson .... paperback $9.95

IOWA'S EARLY HOME REMEDIES
      by 26 students at Wapello Elem. School .... paperback $9.95

IOWA - A JOURNEY IN A PROMISED LAND
      by Kathy Yoder .... paperback $16.95

LOST & BURIED TREASURE OF THE MISSOURI RIVER
      by Netha Bell .... paperback $9.95

FIELD GUIDE TO IOWA'S CRITTERS
      by Bruce Carlson .... paperback $7.95

OLD IOWA HOUSES, YOUNG LOVES
      by Bruce Carlson .... paperback $9.95

SKUNK RIVER ANTHOLOGY
      by Gene Olson .... paperback $9.95

VACANT LOT, SCHOOL YARD & BACK ALLEY GAMES
      by various authors .... paperback $9.95

HOW TO TALK MIDWESTERN
      by Robert Thomas .... paperback $7.95

KANSAS BOOKS

HOW TO TALK KANSAS .... paperback $7.95

STOPOVER IN KANSAS
      by Jon McAlpin .... paperback $9.95

LET'S US GO DOWN TO THE RIVER 'N ...
      by various authors .... paperback $9.95

LOST & BURIED TREASURE OF THE MISSOURI RIVER
      by Netha Bell .... paperback $9.95

101 WAYS TO USE A DEAD RIVER FLY
by Bruce Carlson .... paperback $7.95
VACANT LOT, SCHOOL YARD & BACK ALLEY GAMES
by various authors .... paperback $9.95
HOW TO TALK MIDWESTERN
by Robert Thomas .... paperback $7.95

KENTUCKY BOOKS

GHOSTS OF THE OHIO RIVER (from Pittsburgh to Cincinnati)
by Bruce Carlson .... paperback $9.95
GHOSTS OF THE OHIO RIVER (from Cincinnati to Louisville)
by Bruce Carlson .... paperback $9.95
TALES OF HACKETT'S CREEK
by Dan Titus .... paperback $9.95
LOST & BURIED TREASURE OF THE MISSISSIPPI RIVER
by Netha Bell & Gary Scholl .... paperback $9.95
LET'S US GO DOWN TO THE RIVER 'N ...
by various authors .... paperback $9.95
UNSOLVED MYSTERIES OF THE MISSISSIPPI
by Netha Bell .... paperback $9.95
101 WAYS TO USE A DEAD RIVER FLY
by Bruce Carlson .... paperback $7.95
TALL TALES OF THE MISSISSIPPI RIVER
by Dan Titus .... paperback $9.95
MY VERY FIRST
by various authors .... paperback $9.95
VACANT LOT, SCHOOL YARD & BACK ALLEY GAMES
by various authors .... paperback $9.95

MICHIGAN BOOKS

MICHIGAN COOKIN'
by Bruce Carlson .... (3x5) paperback $5.95
MICHIGAN'S ROADKILL COOKBOOK
by Bruce Carlson .... paperback $7.95
MICHIGAN'S VANISHING OUTHOUSE
by Bruce Carlson .... paperback $9.95

MINNESOTA BOOKS

MINNESOTA'S ROADKILL COOKBOOK
  by Bruce Carlson .... paperback $7.95
REVENGE OF ROADKILL
  by Bruce Carlson .... paperback $7.95
A FIELD GUIDE TO SMALL MINNESOTA FEMALES
  by Bruce Carlson .... paperback $9.95
GHOSTS OF THE MISSISSIPPI RIVER (from Minneapolis to Dubuque)
  by Bruce Carlson .... paperback $9.95
LAKES COUNTRY COOKBOOK
  by Bruce Carlson .... paperback $11.95
UNSOLVED MYSTERIES OF THE MISSISSIPPI
  by Netha Bell .... paperback $9.95
TALES OF HACKETT'S CREEK
  by Dan Titus .... paperback $9.95
GHOSTS OF SOUTHWEST MINNESOTA
  by Ruth Hein .... paperback $9.95
HOW TO TALK LIKE A MINNESOTA NATIVE .... paperback $7.95
MINNESOTA'S VANISHING OUTHOUSE
  by Bruce Carlson .... paperback $9.95
TALL TALES OF THE MISSISSIPPI RIVER
  by Dan Titus .... paperback $9.95
Some Pretty Tame, but Kinda Funny Stories About Early
MINNESOTA LADIES-OF-THE-EVENING   .
  by Bruce Carlson .... paperback $9.95
101 WAYS TO USE A DEAD RIVER FLY .... paperback $7.95
LOST & BURIED TREASURE OF THE MISSISSIPPI RIVER
  by Netha Bell & Gary Scholl .... paperback $9.95
VACANT LOT, SCHOOL YARD & BACK ALLEY GAMES
  by various authors .... paperback $9.95
HOW TO TALK MIDWESTERN
  by Robert Thomas .... paperback $7.95
MINNESOTA COOKIN'
  by Bruce Carlson .... (3x5) paperback $5.95

MISSOURI BOOKS

MISSOURI COOKIN'
  by Bruce Carlson .... (3x5) paperback $5.95
MISSOURI'S ROADKILL COOKBOOK
  by Bruce Carlson .... paperback $7.95

REVENGE OF ROADKILL
 by Bruce Carlson .... paperback $7.95
LET'S US GO DOWN TO THE RIVER 'N ...
 by various authors .... paperback $9.95
LAKES COUNTRY COOKBOOK
 by Bruce Carlson .... paperback $11.95
101 WAYS TO USE A DEAD RIVER FLY
 by Bruce Carlson .... paperback $7.95
TALL TALES OF THE MISSISSIPPI RIVER
 by Dan Titus .... paperback $9.95
TALES OF HACKETT'S CREEK
 by Dan Titus .... paperback $9.95
STRANGE FOLKS ALONG THE MISSISSIPPI
 by Pat Wallace .... paperback $9.95
LOST & BURIED TREASURE OF THE MISSOURI RIVER
 by Netha Bell .... paperback $9.95
HOW TO TALK MISSOURIAN
 by Bruce Carlson .... paperback $7.95
VACANT LOT, SCHOOL YARD & BACK ALLEY GAMES
 by various authors .... paperback $9.95
HOW TO TALK MIDWESTERN
 by Robert Thomas .... paperback $7.95
UNSOLVED MYSTERIES OF THE MISSISSIPPI
 by Netha Bell .... paperback $9.95
LOST & BURIED TREASURE OF THE MISSISSIPPI RIVER
 by Netha Bell & Gary Scholl .... paperback $9.95
MISSISSIPPI RIVER PO' FOLK
 by Pat Wallace .... paperback $9.95
Some Pretty Tame, but Kinda Funny Stories About Early
MISSOURI LADIES-OF-THE-EVENING
 by Bruce Carlson .... paperback $9.95
GUNSHOOTIN', WHISKEY DRINKIN', GIRL CHASIN'
STORIES OUT OF THE OLD MISSOURI TERRITORY
 by Bruce Carlson .... paperback $9.95
THE VANISHING OUTHOUSE OF MISSOURI
 by Bruce Carlson .... paperback $9.95
A FIELD GUIDE TO MISSOURI'S CRITTERS
 by Bruce Carlson .... paperback $7.95
EARLY MISSOURI HOME REMEDIES
 by various authors .... paperback $9.95
GHOSTS OF THE OZARKS
 by Bruce Carlson .... paperback $9.95

MISSISSIPPI RIVER COOKIN' BOOK
    by Bruce Carlson .... paperback $11.95
MISSOURI'S OLD HOUSES, AND NEW LOVES
    by Bruce Carlson .... paperback $9.95
UNDERGROUND MISSOURI
    by Bruce Carlson .... paperback $9.95

NEBRASKA BOOKS

LOST & BURIED TREASURE OF THE MISSOURI RIVER
    by Netha Bell .... paperback $9.95
101 WAYS TO USE A DEAD RIVER FLY
    by Bruce Carlson .... paperback $7.95
LET'S US GO DOWN TO THE RIVER 'N ...
    by various authors .... paperback $9.95
HOW TO TALK MIDWESTERN
    by Robert Thomas .... paperback $7.95
VACANT LOT, SCHOOL YARD & BACK ALLEY GAMES
    by various authors .... paperback $9.95

TENNESSEE BOOKS

TALES OF HACKETT'S CREED
    by Dan Titus .... paperback $9.95
TALL TALES OF THE MISSISSIPPI RIVER
    by Dan Titus .... paperback $9.95
UNSOLVED MYSTERIES OF THE MISSISSIPPI
    by Netha Bell .... paperback $9.95
LOST & BURIED TREASURE OF THE MISSISSIPPI RIVER
    by Netha Bell & Gary Scholl .... paperback $9.95
LET'S US GO DOWN TO THE RIVER 'N ...
    by various authors .... paperback $9.95
101 WAYS TO USE A DEAD RIVER FLY
    by Bruce Carlson .... paperback $7.95
VACANT LOT, SCHOOL YARD & BACK ALLEY GAMES
    by various authors .... paperback $9.95

WISCONSIN BOOKS

HOW TO TALK WISCONSIN .... paperback $7.95
WISCONSIN COOKIN'
     by Bruce Carlson .... (3x5) paperback $5.95
WISCONSIN'S ROADKILL COOKBOOK
     by Bruce Carlson .... paperback $7.95
REVENGE OF ROADKILL
     by Bruce Carlson .... paperback $7.95
TALL TALES OF THE MISSISSIPPI RIVER
     by Dan Titus .... paperback $9.95
LAKES COUNTRY COOKBOOK
     by Bruce Carlson .... paperback $11.95
TALES OF HACKETT'S CREEK
     by Dan Titus .... paperback $9.95
LET'S US GO DOWN TO THE RIVER 'N ...
     by various authors .... paperback $9.95
101 WAYS TO USE A DEAD RIVER FLY
     by Bruce Carlson .... paperback $7.95
UNSOLVED MYSTERIES OF THE MISSISSIPPI
     by Netha Bell .... paperback $9.95
LOST & BURIED TREASURE OF THE MISSISSIPPI RIVER
     by Netha Bell & Gary Scholl .... paperback $9.95
GHOSTS OF THE MISSISSIPPI RIVER (from Dubuque to Keokuk)
     by Bruce Carlson .... paperback $9.95
HOW TO TALK MIDWESTERN
     by Robert Thomas .... paperback $7.95
VACANT LOT, SCHOOL YARD & BACK ALLEY GAMES
     by various authors .... paperback $9.95
MY VERY FIRST
     by various authors .... paperback $9.95
EARLY WISCONSIN HOME REMEDIES
     by various authors .... paperback $9.95
GHOSTS OF THE MISSISSIPPI RIVER (from Minneapolis to Dubuque)
     by Bruce Carlson .... paperback $9.95
THE VANISHING OUTHOUSE OF WISCONSIN
     by Bruce Carlson .... paperback $9.95
GHOSTS OF DOOR COUNTY, WISCONSIN
     by Geri Rider .... paperback $9.95
Some Pretty Tame, but Kinda Funny Stories About Early
WISCONSIN LADIES-OF-THE-EVENING
     by Bruce Carlson .... paperback $9.95

MIDWESTERN BOOKS

A FIELD GUIDE TO THE MIDWEST'S WORST RESTAURANTS
         by Bruce Carlson .... paperback $5.95
THE MOTORIST'S FIELD GUIDE TO MIDWESTERN FARM
EQUIPMENT (misguided information as only a city slicker can give it)
         by Bruce Carlson .... paperback $5.95
VACANT LOT, SCHOOL YARD & BACK ALLEY GAMES
OF THE MIDWEST YEARS AGO
         by various authors .... paperback $9.95
MIDWEST SMALL TOWN COOKING
         by Bruce Carlson .... (3x5) paperback $5.95
HITCHHIKING THE UPPER MIDWEST
         by Bruce Carlson .... paperback $7.95
101 WAYS FOR MIDWESTERNERS TO "DO IN" THEIR
NEIGHBOR'S PESKY DOG WITHOUT GETTING CAUGHT
         by Bruce Carlson .... paperback $5.95

RIVER BOOKS

ON THE SHOULDERS OF A GIANT
         by M. Cody and D. Walker .... paperback $9.95
SKUNK RIVER ANTHOLOGY
         by Gene "Will" Olson .... paperback $9.95
JACK KING vs. DETECTIVE MACKENZIE
         by Netha Bell .... paperback $9.95
LOST & BURIED TREASURES ALONG THE MISSISSIPPI
         by Netha Bell & Gary Scholl .... paperback $9.95
MISSISSIPPI RIVER PO' FOLK
         by Pat Wallace .... paperback $9.95
STRANGE FOLKS ALONG THE MISSISSIPPI
         by Pat Wallace .... paperback $9.95
GHOSTS OF THE OHIO RIVER (from Pittsburgh to Cincinnati)
         by Bruce Carlson .... paperback $9.95
GHOSTS OF THE OHIO RIVER (from Cincinnati to Louisville)
         by Bruce Carlson .... paperback $9.95
GHOSTS OF THE MISSISSIPPI RIVER (Minneapolis to Dubuque)
         by Bruce Carlson .... paperback $9.95
GHOSTS OF THE MISSISSIPPI RIVER (Dubuque to Keokuk)
         by Bruce Carlson .... paperback $9.95
TALL TALES OF THE MISSISSIPPI RIVER
         by Dan Titus .... paperback $9.95

TALL TALES OF THE MISSOURI RIVER
        by Dan Titus .... paperback $9.95
RIVER SHARKS & SHENANIGANS
    (tales of riverboat gambling of years ago)
        by Netha Bell .... paperback $9.95
UNSOLVED MYSTERIES OF THE MISSISSIPPI
        by Netha Bell .... paperback $9.95
TALES OF HACKETT'S CREEK (1940s Mississippi River kids)
        by Dan Titus .... paperback $9.95
101 WAYS TO USE A DEAD RIVER FLY
        by Bruce Carlson .... paperback $7.95
LET'S US GO DOWN TO THE RIVER 'N ...
        by various authors .... paperback $9.95
LOST & BURIED TREASURE OF THE MISSOURI
        by Netha Bell .... paperback $9.95

COOKBOOKS

ROARING 20's COOKBOOK
        by Bruce Carlson .... paperback $11.95
DEPRESSION COOKBOOK
        by Bruce Carlson .... paperback $11.95
LAKES COUNTRY COOKBOOK
        by Bruce Carlson .... paperback $11.95
A COOKBOOK FOR THEM WHAT AIN'T DONE A LOT OF COOKIN'
        by Bruce Carlson .... paperback $11.95
FLAT-OUT DIRT-CHEAP COOKIN' COOKBOOK
        by Bruce Carlson .... paperback $11.95
APHRODISIAC COOKING
        by Bruce Carlson .... paperback $11.95
WILD CRITTER COOKBOOK
        by Bruce Carlson .... paperback $11.95
I GOT FUNNIER-THINGS-TO-DO-THAN-COOKIN' COOKBOOK
        by Louise Lum .... paperback $11.95
MISSISSIPPI RIVER COOKIN' BOOK
        by Bruce Carlson .... paperback $11.95
HUNTING IN THE NUDE COOKBOOK
        by Bruce Carlson .... paperback $9.95
DAKOTA COOKIN'
        by Bruce Carlson .... (3x5) paperback $5.95
IOWA COOKIN'
        by Bruce Carlson .... (3x5) paperback $5.95

MICHIGAN COOKIN'
      by Bruce Carlson .... (3x5) paperback $5.95
MINNESOTA COOKIN'
      by Bruce Carlson .... (3x5) paperback $5.95
MISSOURI COOKIN'
      by Bruce Carlson .... (3x5) paperback $5.95
ILLINOIS COOKIN'
      by Bruce Carlson .... (3x5) paperback $5.95
WISCONSIN COOKIN'
      by Bruce Carlson .... (3x5) paperback $5.95
HILL COUNTRY COOKIN'
      by Bruce Carlson .... (3x5) paperback $5.95
MIDWEST SMALL TOWN COOKIN'
      by Bruce Carlson .... (3x5) paperback $5.95
APHRODISIAC COOKIN'
      by Bruce Carlson .... (3x5) paperback $5.95
PREGNANT LADY COOKIN'
      by Bruce Carlson .... (3x5) paperback $5.95
GOOD COOKIN' FROM THE PLAIN PEOPLE
      by Bruce Carlson .... (3x5) paperback $5.95
WORKING GIRL COOKING
      by Bruce Carlson .... (3x5) paperback $5.95
COOKING FOR ONE
      by Barb.Layton .... paperback $11.95
SUPER SIMPLE COOKING
      by Barb Layton .... (3x5) paperback $5.95
OFF TO COLLEGE COOKBOOK
      by Barb Layton .... (3x5) paperback $5.95
COOKING WITH THINGS THAT GO SPLASH
      by Bruce Carlson .... (3x5) paperback $5.95
COOKING WITH THINGS THAT GO MOO
      by Bruce Carlson .... (3x5) paperback $5.95
COOKING WITH SPIRITS
      by Bruce Carlson .... (3x5) paperback $5.95
INDIAN COOKING COOKBOOK
      by Bruce Carlson .... paperback $9.95
DIAL-A-DREAM COOKBOOK
      by Bruce Carlson .... (3x5) paperback $5.95
HORMONE HELPER COOKBOOK .... (3x5) paperback $5.95

MISCELLANEOUS BOOKS

DEAR TABBY (letters to and from a feline advice columnist)
        by Bruce Carlson .... paperback $5.95
HOW TO BEHAVE (etiquette advice for non-traditional
and awkward circumstances such as attending dogfights,
what to do when your blind date turns out to be your spouse, etc.)
        by Bruce Carlson .... paperback $5.95
REVENGE OF THE ROADKILL
        by Bruce Carlson .... paperback $7.95